CHAIN MAILLE JEWELLERY

Handmade Designs and Techniques

CHAIN MAILLE JEWELLERY

Handmade Designs and Techniques

33 creative step-by-step jewellery
projects made from jump rings

Olive Nettle

For Matt, Freya & Kyra

CONTENTS

Introduction 8
Tools and Materials 9
Techniques 15
Loosing your place in the weave 17

Chapter one: Working with jump rings 18

Chapter two: Byzantine Weave 21

Byzantine Love Chain Bracelet 24
Berry Bush Cuff 26
Citrine Clustered Earrings 32
Triple Link Byzantine Ring 35
Square Rings Dangly Earrings 37
Byzantine Earrings Design Variation 40

Chapter three: European 4 in 1 Weave 43

European 4 in 1 Chain Collar 46
Inverted Triangle Collar 48
European 4 in 1 Jewellery Set 54
Choker 55
Necklace 60
Dangly Earrings 63
Florets Chain Collar 65
Star Pendant Choker 68
Sunflower Pendant Choker 72
Knotted European 4 in 1 Drop Earrings 76
Diamond Copper Ring 80
Knotted European 4 in 1 Heart Bracelet 84

Chapter four: Dragonscale Weave 87
Dragonscale Bracelet 94
Pine Cone Earrings and A Necklace 97
Citrine Rough Nuggets Lantern 104
Dragonscale Flower Collar 108

Chapter five: Mobius Weave 111
Nest Bracelet with
Rhinestone Butterfly Charms 113
Mobius Jewellery Set 116
Mobius Link Bracelet 117
Mobius Link Dangly Earrings 119
Mobius Link Necklace 121

Chapter six: Box Weave 123
Graduated Mesh Collar with Pearls 128
Tunnel Chain Necklace 133
Triple Strand Bracelet 136
Inverted Cone Dangly Earrings 138
Peacock Earrings 141
Golden Eye Bracelet 144
Gold Feather Earrings 149

INTRODUCTION

CHAIN MAILLE

What is chain maille?

Chain maille is made up of jump rings linked to one another to create a flexible pattern. The invention of chain maille as part of the armour acts as a defence during the middle ages. In today's generation, It still has many uses; used as costumes, protection from shark bites, made as cut-resistant items and **jewellery pieces.**

Over the past few years, chain maille has become one of the very favourite techniques in jewellery making. With the use of jump rings and a few tools, one can link a pattern together one at a time and create a unique piece of wearable art.

The collection represents my favourite works produced with the use of jump rings as a foundational element. The productive potential of jump rings possesses as a medium is a proof of the diversity of the work on these pages.

I have included as many photos as possible to illustrate the steps that will guide you with your weave along with simple instructions.

I have divided the book into six chapters. The first chapter is about working with jump rings. Followed by chapters on each of the chain maille weaves used as techniques to create these collections of jewellery. And in some sections, you'll find out that some of the patterns were combined to create a design as it is in this way that they work together to create wonderful pieces of jewellery.

I hope that the designs represented in this book will serve as an inspiration for other artists.

TOOLS AND MATERIALS

In this book, the projects are made using commonly used tools and of materials that are reasonably priced to buy and easy to find. As you flick through each project, you'll see that none of the tools requires a specialist equipment. You just need your jump rings in your chosen sizes and colours, some pliers, a proper lighting and you are all set to get started.

Jump rings

The starting point is to choose your jump rings for the project you will be working. Choosing the right jump rings will make designing an enjoyable experience because the jump rings will be responsible for the weave that you want your jewellery design to be in a constructive and flexible way.

There are now many jump rings sold online or in jewellery shops. Making your jump rings is also a great option. Jump rings are made of different materials, and I suggest you first begin with base metals if you are just starting with chain maille as they are reasonably cheaper to experiment with jewellery designs than precious metals like silver and gold.

Some projects in this book only require one size jump ring, and some are constructed in different jump ring sizes.

Using jump rings is one of the most exciting and interesting ways of creating unique designs of jewellery.

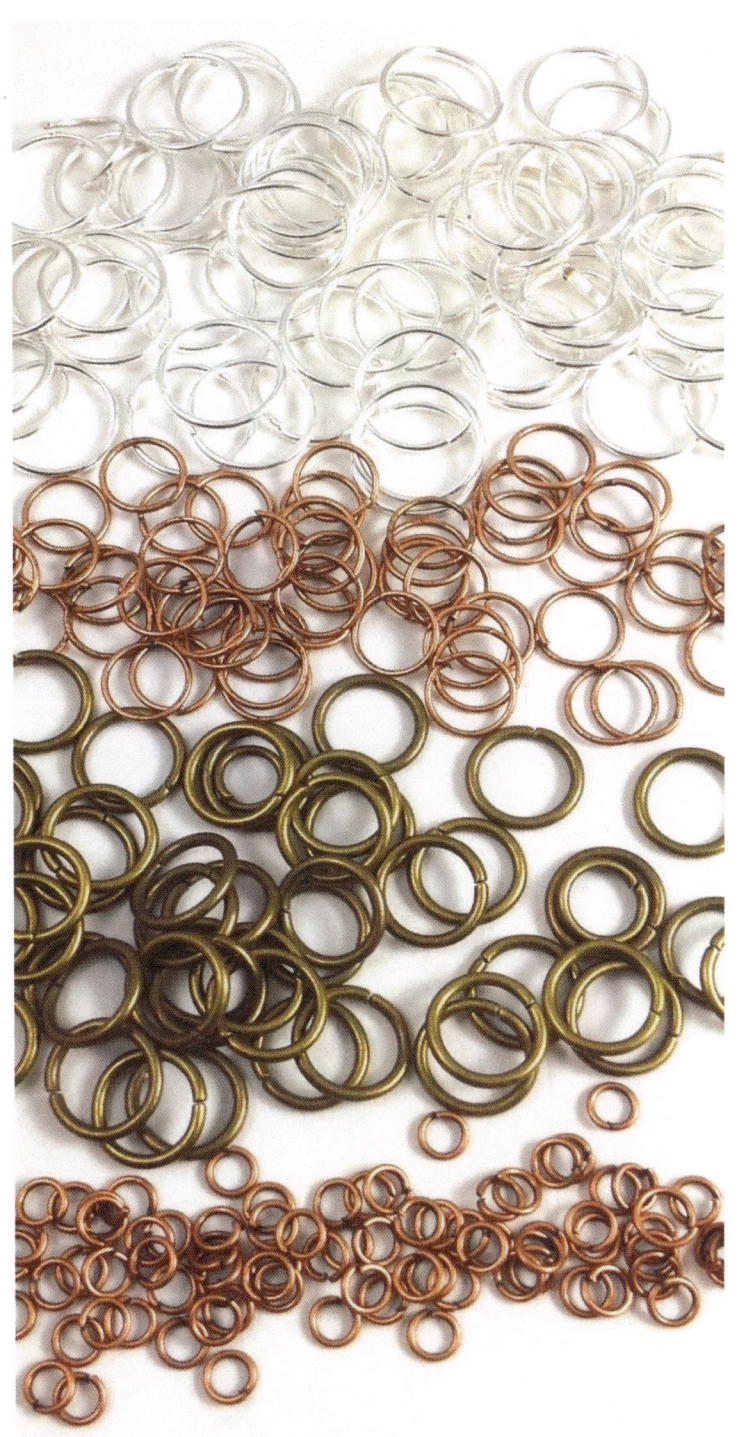

Pliers

Choose pliers that are not necessarily expensive, but it should have certain qualities because working with wrong pliers can be very frustrating.

I find some of the pliers' handle too small or too large for my hand, and it gets uncomfortable to grip. Find something that is best for your working hand that will allow you to work comfortably and more efficiently.

Also, it's best to have a collection of pliers on hand so you can change anytime the need arises. Most of the pliers used in these projects are the following:

1. Flat nose pliers. They have flat, smooth jaws and are used to firmly hold wires and jewellery components while working on them as well as for bending and flattening wire.

2. Chain nose pliers. It's also known as snipe-nose. These pliers have flat jaws that narrow at the end and are useful for holding small pieces of wire and for creating wrapped loops.

3. Round nose pliers. These have round nose jaws that narrow to the end and are used for making jump rings, eye pins, and for forming loops, curves and spirals.

4. Nylon jaw pliers. Similar to flat nose pliers but these have thick nylon-coated jaws that protect precious metal wires and components against scratches and dents. It's also useful for straightening wires that are bent or kinked with the help of another pair of pliers.

5. Side cutters. These cutters have the cutting jaw at the side, angled for a clean, flush cut and used for cutting soft wires.

6. Bent nose pliers. These have fine tips that are bent to one side allowing you to access small areas that are difficult to reach.

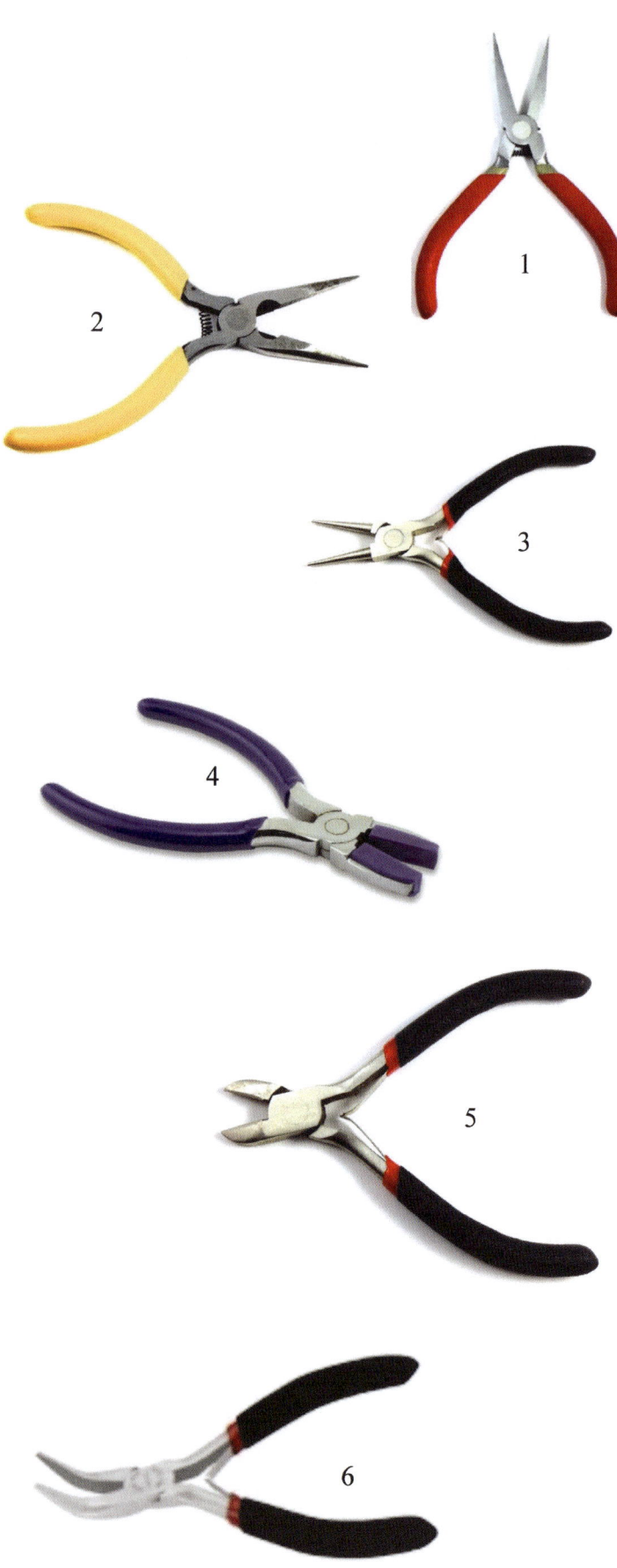

Measuring Tools

Two of the measuring tools used in these projects to measure the Inside Diameter (ID) and a Wire Diameter (WD) or Gauge of a jump ring are Digital Calliper and Standard Wire Gauge (SWG)

Digital Calliper

It has an internal and external measuring jaws that measures the dimensions of an object by placing it in a particular section where it fits, then slide the calliper to open. It shows measurement in either inches or metric digits on the screen.

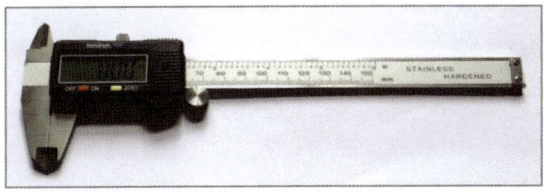

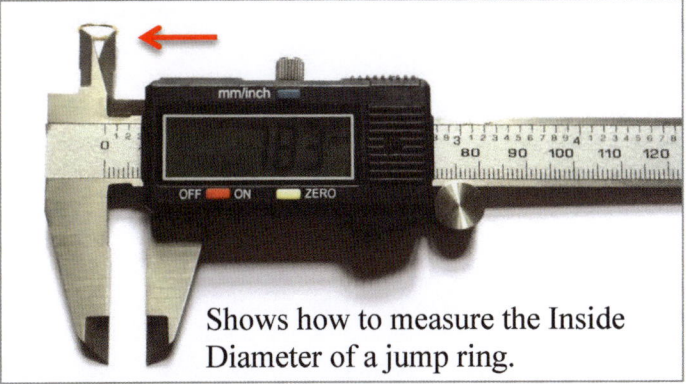

Shows how to measure the Inside Diameter of a jump ring.

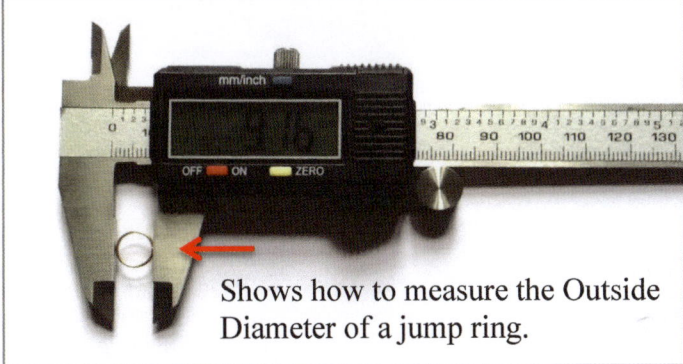

Shows how to measure the Outside Diameter of a jump ring.

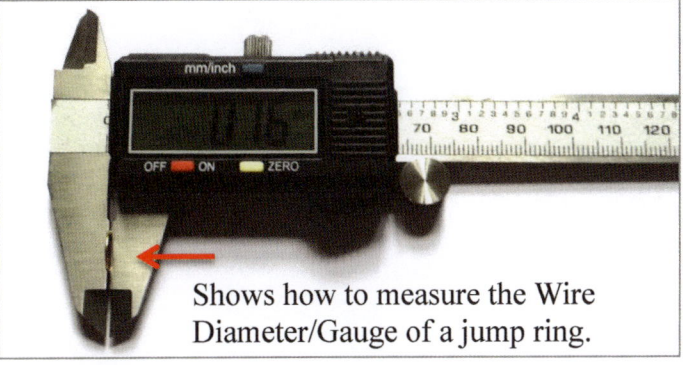

Shows how to measure the Wire Diameter/Gauge of a jump ring.

Standard Wire Gauge (SWG)

It is also known as Imperial Wire Gauge or British Standard Gauge used in the UK and Europe.

This measuring tool is a circle with slots around the perimeter in graduated sizes to insert a wire. Each slot tells you a particular size or gauge. The gauges run from zero at the largest end to 36 at the smallest end.

Another wire gauge standard is also called American Wire Gauge (AWG) Otherwise known as the Brown and Sharpe Standard and widely used to measure a wire for its wire diameter in the US and Canada.

SWG is not to be confused with American Wire Gauge (AWG) which has a similar but not entirely interchangeable numbering scheme, so when measuring your jump rings, remember to write it down whether it's either AWG or SWG for future use and or reference.

Front shows measurement in Gauge

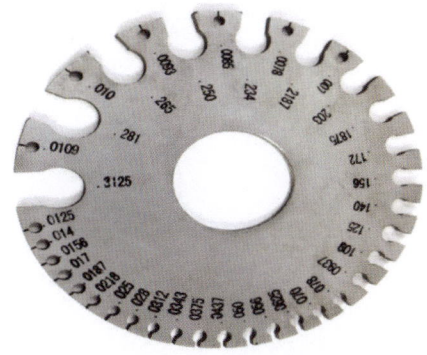

Back shows equivalent measurement of gauge in either inches or millimeters

Embellishments

Although chain maille jewellery is stunning in itself, you can also add extra feature or detail to make it look unique and attractive.

Beads

There are various types of beads you can choose from depending upon your design. There's wooden beads, glass beads, metal beads, pearl beads, semi-precious gemstone beads, etc. In this book, I've mostly used freshwater pearls and semi-precious gemstones.

Crystals

There's a huge range of beautiful crystals to satisfy your jewellery making needs. They add sparkle and glamour to your designs. Pick whichever suits your taste and style. I have used Swarovski Elements in my designs as it adds elegance and brightness.

Charms and Pendants

Another way to make your jewellery designs exciting is to add fashionable charms and pendants. There's plenty of choices out there to suit your taste like Diamante, metal, resin, ceramic, etc. In page 113 of this book, I have added rhinestone butterfly charms in my Mobius link bracelet to add colour and shine to the design.

Findings

These are a fundamental part of jewellery making as they make your designs safe, secure and stunning.

Eye pins

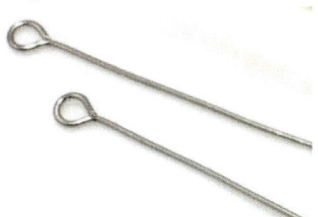

A piece of wire with a loop at one end used for threading your beads. The loop can be opened to attach it to your piece and closed back again.

Ear wires

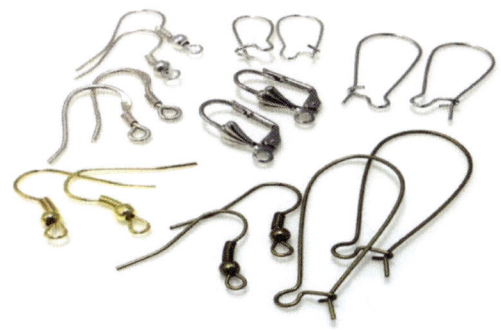

Ear wires are perfect for making a full range of gorgeous earrings from classic to contemporary, and they come in an extensive range of styles.

Clasps

Clasps are an essential element in making your jewellery designs. Their primary function is to join your beautifully handcrafted piece of jewellery together and make them wearable. They come in wide range of sizes, colours, styles and qualities. And I love using them not just for attaching my pieces together but as focal points of my designs too. See page 14.

13

1. Lobster Clasps

This type of clasps suits all kinds of jewellery. It's perfect for securely fastening your piece and, it's tidy and not fussy.

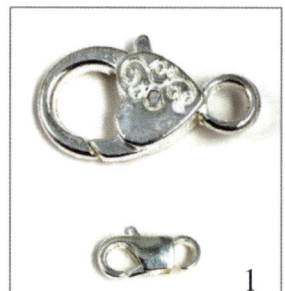
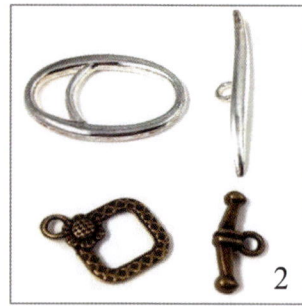

2. Toggle Clasps

Apart from just securely locking your design, this type of clasps is an excellent use as a focal point of your designs or to accentuate their beauty. They come in a vast range of colours, shapes and sizes from simple and plain to understated elegant and fancy look.

3. Multi-Strand Clasps

These fasteners are made especially for jewellery designs with more than just one strand and are fashioned to slide and lock inside of each other for a safe and secure finish and ensures that the strands are attached neatly and also sits perfectly.

4. Push Button Clasps/Box Clasps

These multi-stranded push button traditional style fasteners are ideal for adding a beautiful vintage look to your handmade designs, and a fantastic way to have a professional finish to your multi-stranded necklaces and bracelets.

5. S Hook Clasps or J-Hook and Eye Clasps

Finish off your jewellery designs elegantly and professionally with this clasp. It is a classic method of connecting jewellery designs and adds a touch of a vintage look to your pieces. It's straightforward to use by just attaching the end of your chain to the loop on your hook and the other end to the eye. It is ideal for people who find lobster clasps, or bolt ring clasps not easy to use.

6. Bolt Ring Clasps

It is designed to have a spring mechanism which allows the trigger to close itself after you pull the lever back.

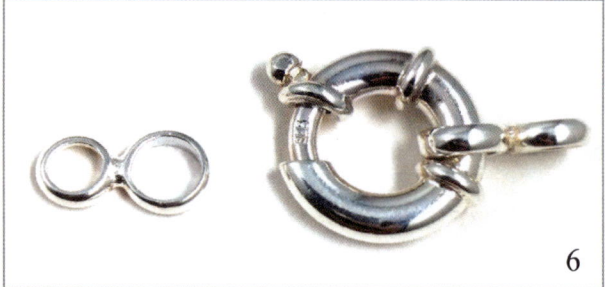

TECHNIQUES

Basic techniques to get you started with your projects

OPENING AND CLOSING JUMP RINGS

STEP ONE

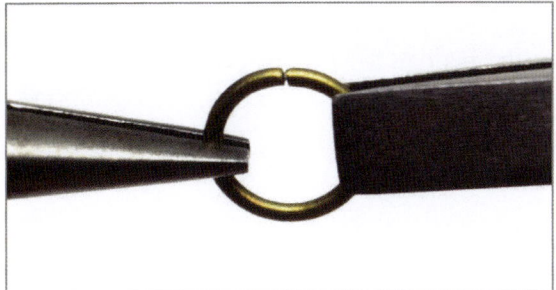

Position your pliers on each side of the jump ring between its opening. You can either use two pairs of flat nose pliers or a couple of a flat nose and chain nose pliers.

STEP TWO

To open the jump ring, gently move a pair of pliers toward you. Never pull both ends apart as it will affect the shape of your jump ring.

You can also position your left-hand pliers vertically as shown above for a better grip when opening and closing your jump rings.

STEP THREE

To close the jump ring, reverse back the action of your pliers by pulling the jump ring away from you and bring the ends neatly back together.

FORMING A PLAIN LOOP

STEP ONE

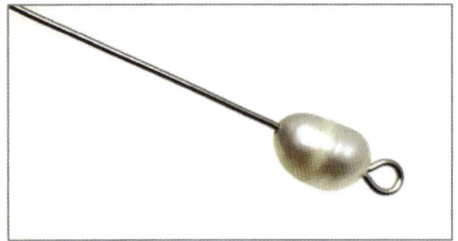

Thread your bead on an eye pin, headpin or a piece of wire.

STEP TWO

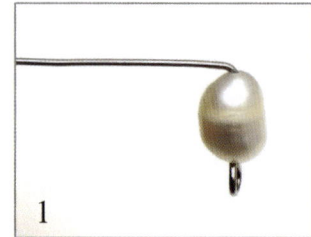

Bend the wire above the bead at a 90-degree angle using your finger or a pair of chain nose or flat nose pliers, then trim the excess wire with your wire cutter.

STEP THREE

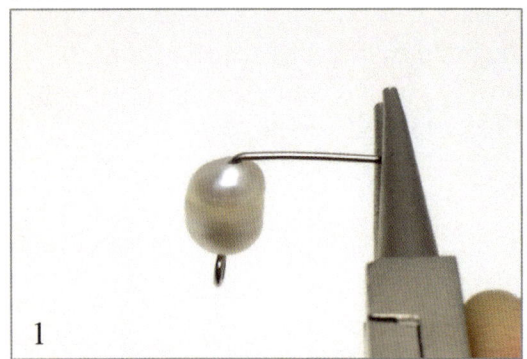

Position your round nose pliers at the end of the wire and to the size which you like your loop to be. Rotate the pliers towards the bead as it curls. Reposition your round nose pliers as you continue rotating your wire until the loop forms. It's now ready to be attached to other components.

LOOSING YOUR PLACE IN THE WEAVE

Whether you're a beginner or an expert, there are tendencies to lose your concentration, make mistakes in the process and lose your place in the weave. One of the many reasons can merely be a distraction from a neighbour knocking at your door or a phone call. Or only just new to the pattern and got you confused along the way.

WHAT CAN YOU DO?

Find your place again

Don't feel upset and don't give up! Double-check your work and try and turn your piece at different angles. In this way, you'll be able to find where your mistake is and where did the error happen. Sometimes, you'll be surprised that there is no mistake and it did just look wrong because it's not in the right position. But if you found some errors, unpick few links from your weave to help you get back into the correct place again.

Unpick back to the mistake

If you made a mistake and lost your place at the beginning of the weave, find the error and put a piece of wire to mark it. Unpick the links until you are back to the right place again.

Unpick up to the mistake

You're just about to finish your chain when you noticed that you made an error at the beginning of your weave. Just continue and complete your work then go back to where the mistake is and put a piece of wire only after the error. Unpick the first link right up to the mistake. Use the unpicked jump rings to finish your chain.

Mark your place

If for some reason you need to stop your weave, take a piece of wire and twist around the area where you have stopped the link, this will quickly help you pick where you left off.

chapter one

WORKING WITH JUMP RINGS

Jump rings are a significant part of jewellery making. We always need a jump ring whether we want to add a charm or to add length to our clasp. They enfold our designs together and allow us to enhance and beautify them in countless ways. And in this book, they are the very foundation of my designs.

When working with jump rings, I do tend to be more adventurous, and this is where I make a lot of mistakes. I experiment with any size of jump rings to start a design hoping it will work well on a particular weave and at times this leads me to either too loose or too tight weave. But it's also an excellent way to learn and improve. Furthermore, this experiment usually prompts me to a beautiful, unexpected design and fortunately, when making mistakes with jump rings, you can always re-use them for a later project.

JUMP RING MATERIALS
Jump rings are available in different metals and come in various sizes, colours and shapes.

METALS
Base metals are the primary metallic element in an alloy. A common and widely used metal in commercial and industrial use as it's far cheaper and readily available than precious metals like silver, gold and platinum.

Bronze and copper jump rings are sturdy, and they add a unique shine to your designs.

Brass and plated brass jump rings are economical. Plated brass jump rings come in a variety of metal finishes like antique silver, gunmetal and more.

Aluminium jump rings are very light in weight and come in an array of colours. Use this to add more colour to your designs.

Precious metals are elements that are valuable and rare. Gold is known for its unique yellow colour, malleability and conductivity. Silver is known for its high electrical and thermal conductivity and is used popularly for jewellery. It is also well valued for its beauty. Platinum is dense and malleable. Due to its rarity and it's excellent resistance to corrosion, it makes the most precious metals amongst other precious metals.

Sterling silver jump rings are a perfect choice for higher quality designs. They are more expensive due to its value as a precious metal. They have shiny, smooth and semi-hypoallergenic qualities. They are composed of 92.5% silver and a 7.5% mixture of other metals (mainly copper) to strengthen it and to slow down the tarnishing process. Fine silver is 99.9% pure silver but not suitable for chain maille as it's relatively soft and can easily bend or break.

Gold filled jump rings are an excellent high-quality alternative to pure gold as it offers all the same characteristics such as strength, durability and beauty at a much more affordable price. They have a high value, are tarnish resistant, semi-hypoallergenic, and they do not flake off or turn colours which can happen to plated jump rings. Gold-filled is composed of an actual layer of gold-pressure bonded to another metal.

SHAPES
Apart from the usual round jump rings, you can also add unique shapes to your designs like ovals, squares and triangles.

SIZES

Measure your jump ring sizes with the use of measuring tools (See page 11). It is essential to know which parts of the jump ring to measure.

Body Parts of a Jump Ring

There are three main parts of a jump ring - a *Wire Diameter or Gauge, The Inside Diameter* and *The Outside Diameter.* When measuring jump rings, it is essential to keep in mind these three.

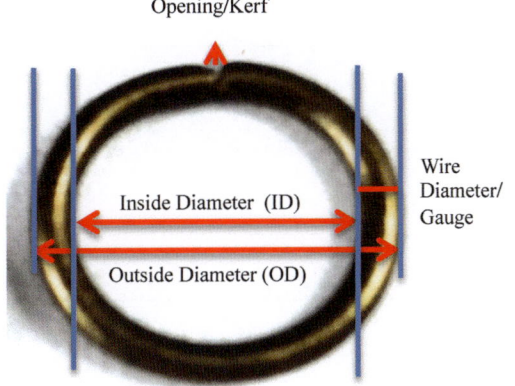

Jump Ring Measurement

Some jump ring vendors or suppliers measure their jump rings based on Inside Diameter (ID) or Outside Diameter (OD). So check with them before purchasing.

In chain maille, the right size of jump rings will work best on the design when the Inside Diameter and the Wire Diameter are in the same coherence called Aspect Ratio.

Aspect Ratio (AR)

The relationship between the Inside Diameter (ID) of a jump ring and the Wire diameter (WD) of a jump ring.

How to find the Aspect Ratio?

A simple formula used to locate the Aspect Ratio of a jump ring is by dividing the Inside Diameter (ID) of a jump ring by the Wire Diameter (WD) of a jump ring.

Formula:

INSIDE DIAMETER/WIRE DIAMETER = ASPECT RATIO

OR

ID/WD=AR

Example:

ID 5.34mm / WD 1.52mm = AR 3.51mm

In this example, it shows that a jump ring which measures 5.34mm Inside Diameter and with a 1.52mm Wire Diameter will have an Aspect Ratio of 3.51mm.

Knowing the Aspect Ratio of your jump ring will then give you the chance to alter or vary a design. You can either use a large, thick/thin jump ring or small, thick/thin jump ring to make a design in the same pattern as long as they have the equal Aspect Ratio or falls within the Aspect Ratio.

Some weaves are flexible that it allows you to use a slightly different and not the exact jump ring size. But some projects need the precise jump ring size to work. And this is where knowing the aspect ratio becomes very helpful, as you need not guess which one works for a specific design. It also saves your time looking for the right jump ring size but feel free to experiment as this also allows you to develop a sense of which different jump ring sizes is best for a weave.

SAW CUT, MACHINE CUT AND SHEARS CUT

Jump rings come in either saw-cut, machine-cut or shears-cut. These techniques make such a massive difference in jump rings. So, you have the option to choose whichever type of jump rings to use based on its availability, budget, design, etc.

The saw-cut method is a much-preferred technique as they are designed to cut through a jump ring in an even, level cut. It would make the jump ring close together very tightly without any gap and provides a smoother edge. Due to its high quality, it can be more expensive, but it's well worth it as it makes all the difference to a successful finished design.

Jump rings cut with shears are the first method used, and they usually leave the metal pinched on one or both sides of the cut which causes a rift and prevent the jump ring from closing correctly.

Using a machine to cut jump rings can be much more comfortable, and a faster process but jump rings can have the same pinched ends and a gap as shears-cut jump rings. The quality of jump rings that is shears or machine-cut varies.

KEY TO WIRE GAUGES/DIAMETERS

In the step instructions throughout this book, we will refer to the SWG gauge size. Refer to the conversion chart of the jump ring sizes mainly used in this book. You can see the materials needed to create each project for all conversions.

Wire is measured differently in the UK, US and Canada. American Standard Wire Gauge (AWG) otherwise known as the Brown and Sharpe Standard and widely used to measure a wire for its wire diameter in the US and Canada. Standard Wire Gauge (SWG) or the British Imperial Standard is used to measure in the UK and Europe.

AWG Inches	AWG MM	Gauge	SWG MM	SWG Inches
0.0641	1.63	14	2.03	0.080
0.0571	1.45	15	1.83	0.072
0.0508	1.29	16	1.63	0.064
0.0453	1.15	17	1.42	0.056
0.0403	1.02	18	1.22	0.048
0.0359	0.912	19	1.02	0.040
0.032	0.813	20	0.914	0.036
0.0285	0.724	21	0.813	0.032
0.0253	0.643	22	0.711	0.028
0.0226	0.574	23	0.610	0.024
0.0201	0.511	24	0.559	0.022
0.0179	0.455	25	0.508	0.020
0.0159	0.404	26	0.457	0.0180

Key to Abbreviations

AWG: American Wire Gauge
SWG: Standard Wire Gauge
G: Gauge
MM: Millimeter
AR: Aspect Ratio
ID: Inside Diameter
OD: Outside Diameter
WD: Wire Diameter

chapter two

BYZANTINE WEAVE

This weave is an ancient pattern, and it is excellent as a basis for learning chain maille.

Create your designs and finish it with stylish findings that feature intricate appearance and flexibility.

STEPS TO FOLLOW

STEP ONE

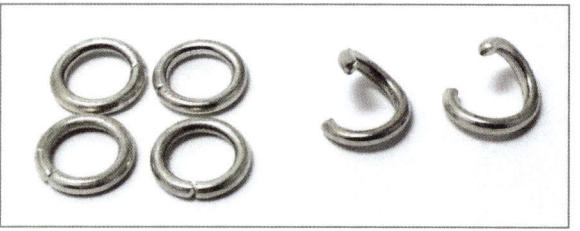  

With one open jump ring, scoop four closed jump ring. Close the jump ring. Double the jump ring. Arrange your rings and notice a 2-2-2 pattern on your weave.

STEP TWO

 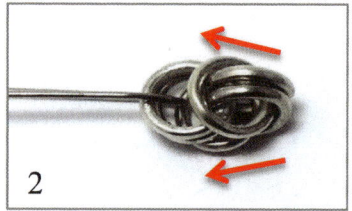

Take a wire and wind it on your first two jump rings to mark where you've started your weave. Arrange your weave. See figure 1. Flip back the last two jump rings, one on to the top and one to the bottom. The two middle jump rings now appear in the front. See figure 2.

STEP THREE

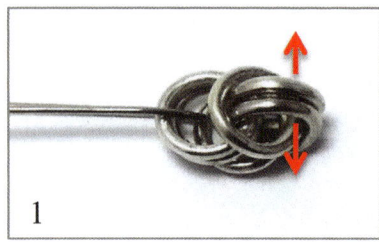 

Open the two front rings wide apart. See figure 1. The tails of the two jump ring flipped in step two appears. See figure 2.

STEP FOUR

Take one open jump ring and attach it to the two tails of both jump rings that appeared in step three (figure1). Close the jump ring (figure 2). Double the jump ring (figure 3).

STEP FIVE

Take one open jump ring and attach it to the two rings connected in step four. Close the ring. Double the ring.

STEP SIX

Once more, take another open jump ring and link it to the two previously attached rings (Figure 1). Close the ring (figure 2). Double the ring. Notice that your weave is now back to 2-2-2 pattern (figure 3).

STEP SEVEN

This time, you're going to flip the last two jump rings sideways and the two middle jump rings appear.

Open the two middle jump rings apart and link two jump rings to the two tails of previously flipped jump rings.

Link two jump rings to the two jump rings just attached. Then connect two more jump rings. You will notice another 2-2-2 pattern. Repeat steps two to seven to finish your desired length.

BYZANTINE LOVE CHAIN BRACELET

One size silver plated jump rings linked one at a time following a Byzantine weave to create this robust and straightforward yet elegant bracelet. It's 7.75 inches long including clasp and loop. Finished with a heart lobster clasp.

TO CREATE YOU WILL NEED

105 silver plated jump rings - 5.34mm ID, 17 gauge
1 heart lobster clasp - 25.78mm(L) x 14.74mm(W)
Chain nose pliers
Flat nose nose pliers

Before you start, open 101 jump rings and leave 4 closed jump rings.

STEPS TO FOLLOW

STEP ONE

Create your chain. Follow steps one-seven on pages 22 and 23. End your chain with one jump ring (figure 2).

STEP TWO

To attach the lobster clasp, re-open the first two jump rings at the other end of your bracelet and connect them to the lobster clasp. Close both rings. (figure 1 and 2)

Finish the bracelet with your choice of a decorative clasp which gives it a unique feature and/or a theme.

BERRY BUSH CUFF

An 8 inch timeless and classic beautiful cuff embellished with an autumn coloured round faceted gemstone beads set in a lovely square shaped Byzantine links. Finished perfectly with a multi-strand clasp.

TO CREATE YOU WILL NEED

1000 silver plated jump rings - 1.97mm ID, 24 gauge
14 silver plated jump rings - 4.99mm ID, 21 gauge
28 round citrine faceted gemstone beads (4.30mm)
28 silver plated eye pins
Sterling silver cylinder 3-strand slider clasp
Chain nose pliers
Flat nose pliers
4 pieces of wire

1. Thread your 28 beads.
2. Open all jump rings.
3. Make each component first then attach it to one another.

STEPS TO FOLLOW

STEP ONE

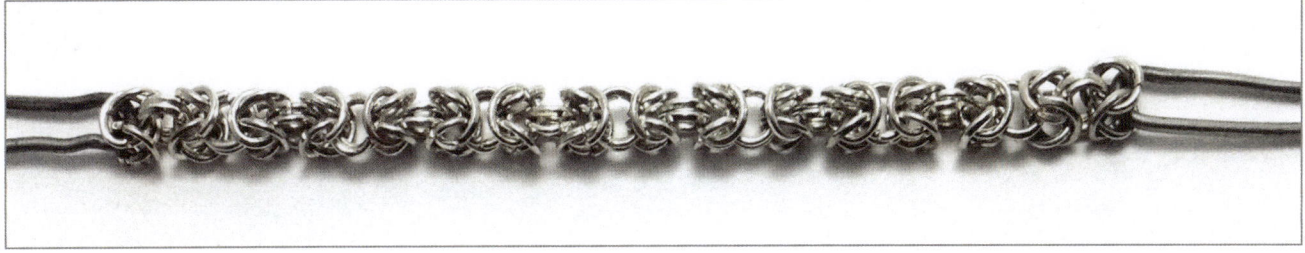

Using 94 open jump rings (1.97mm ID, 24 gauge), create your chain following a byzantine weave on pages 22-23. Use a piece of wire to mark where you began your chain as well as where you've ended. See photo above.

STEP TWO

1

2

3

4

Using the wires as guides, attach the two ends of your chain with one open jump ring (1.97mm ID, 24 gauge) . Close the ring (figure 3). You can now take your wires off. Double the ring (figure 4).

STEP THREE

Arrange your piece into a square shape showing its four outer corners. Use a piece of wire to mark each of these corners. Starting from any of the four corners, link a pair of jump rings (figure 3). Take two more jump rings and connect it to the pair of jump rings just attached. You now have a 2-2-2 chain (figure 4). Weave this chain following steps two-four on page 22 (figure 5). Repeat this procedure to the three remaining corners and your piece should look like in figure 6.

STEP FOUR

In each middle corner between your weaved chains, add your threaded beads. Slightly open one of the eye loop of your threaded bead (*open and close eye loop same as you close and open jump rings. See page 15)* and attach it to each corner. Close the loop. See figure 3.

STEP FIVE

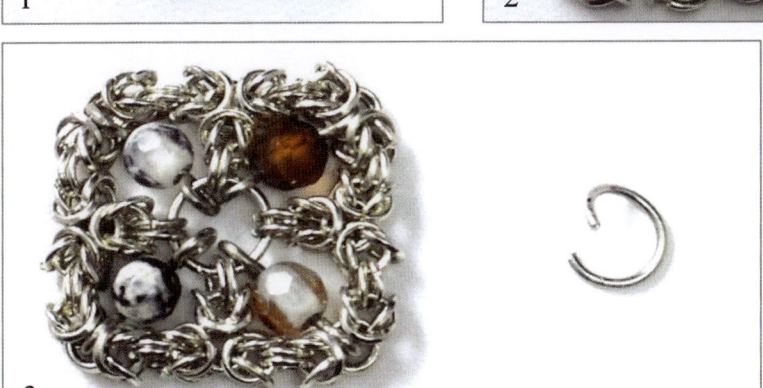

Fold back the weaved rings and the threaded beads into the square. See figure 1. Take one silver plated jump ring (4.99mm ID, 21 gauge) and link it to the threaded beads and weaved rings at the center of the square. Double the ring. Close the ring. See figure 4.

STEP SIX

Connect one open jump ring (1.97mm ID, 24 gauge) on the top right end corner of the square, Close the ring. Double the ring. Take another open jump ring and connect it to the two rings just linked. Close the ring. Double the ring. Again, you'll notice a 2-2-2 chain. See figures 1-4.

STEP SEVEN

Repeat step six to finish the middle and bottom corners on the right side (figure 1-3). Continue with the three corners on the opposite side (figure 4). You've just created your first component with a 2-2-2 chain hanging on six corners.

STEP EIGHT

Repeat steps one-seven to create 6 more components.

STEP NINE

1

2

3

4

5

6

Once you've created all the seven components, start connecting them. To attach, start with a pair of components. Weave your 2-2-2 chain from one corner of each component by flipping back the last two jump rings one on each side. The two middle jump rings then emerge, open the rings and the tails of the first two flipped jump rings appear. Take an open jump ring and link these tails from one component to the other. Close the ring. See figure 1. Double the ring (figure 2). Repeat this step for the next two corners of each component. The two components are now attached. Continue with this step until all seven components are connected. See figures 1-6.

STEP TEN

1

2

3

4

5

6

7

8

9

All components are now connected, so finish the bracelet with your 3-strand slide bar clasp. To join, weave the first bottom end corner of your 2-2-2 chain. Flip the last two jump rings, one onto the top and one to the bottom. The two middle jump rings then appear. Open the rings apart, and the tail of the first two flipped jump rings appears. Take an open jump ring (1.97mm ID, 24 gauge) and attach this to the two tail jump rings then to the first bottom end loop of your clasp. Close the ring. Double the ring. Repeat this step till you have attached all the ends of your bracelet. See figures 1-9.

STEP ELEVEN

Repeat step ten to attach the other pair of your clasp.

CITRINE CLUSTERED EARRINGS

Lovely 2.75 inch long earrings in a chain of Byzantine clustered around warm colour round citrine. Vintage inspired, perfect style for everyday wear.

TO CREATE YOU WILL NEED

244 silver plated jump rings - 2.28mm ID, 21 gauge
6 silver plated eye pins
6 citrine round gemstone beads (4mm)
2 sterling silver ear wire hooks

Chain nose pliers
Flat nose pliers
Round nose pliers
Side cutters

STEPS TO FOLLOW

STEP ONE

Using Byzantine weave, create a chain using 38 jump rings (see pages 22-23). Your chain should finish with the same end. Weave six of these chains.

STEP TWO

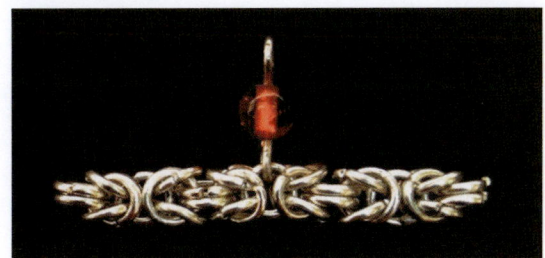

Thread your six beads using an eye pin creating a simple loop (see page 16). At the middle of your first chain, open and attach one loop of your threaded bead. Close the loop.

STEP THREE

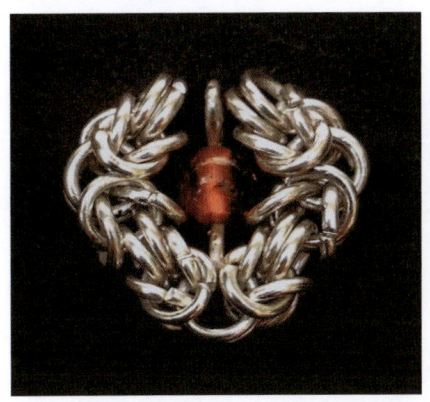 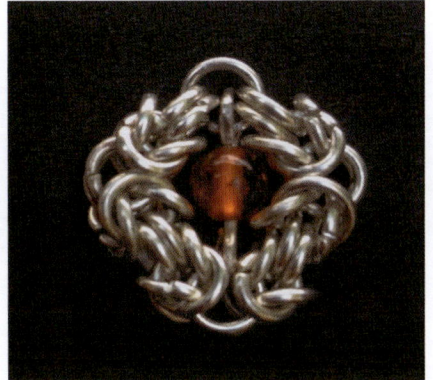

Fold both ends of your chain upwards, so that they both meet at the top in between the loop of your bead. Take one open jump ring and link them all together. Close the ring. Double the ring. This is your first component. Create six of these to make your pair of earrings.

STEP FOUR

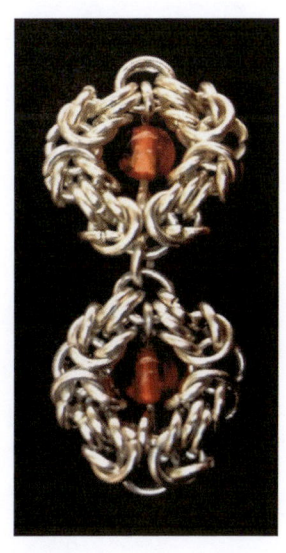

Take three of your components to make the first set of your earrings. Connect each element with two jump rings ensuring they are linked in the same way. See that the direction of the beads is in the same position and so as the bottom part of the components.

STEP FIVE

When the three components are attached, link two jump rings at the top end of the component (figure 1). Take another jump ring and attach it to the ear wire hook then to the two rings just attached (figure 2). Close the ring. Double the jump ring (figure 3). Repeat steps one-five to create the other pair.

Vary your design by just using one or two components each pair.

You can also try different colours of beads and jump rings.

This can also be used as a pendant for a simple chain necklace.

TRIPLE LINK BYZANTINE RING

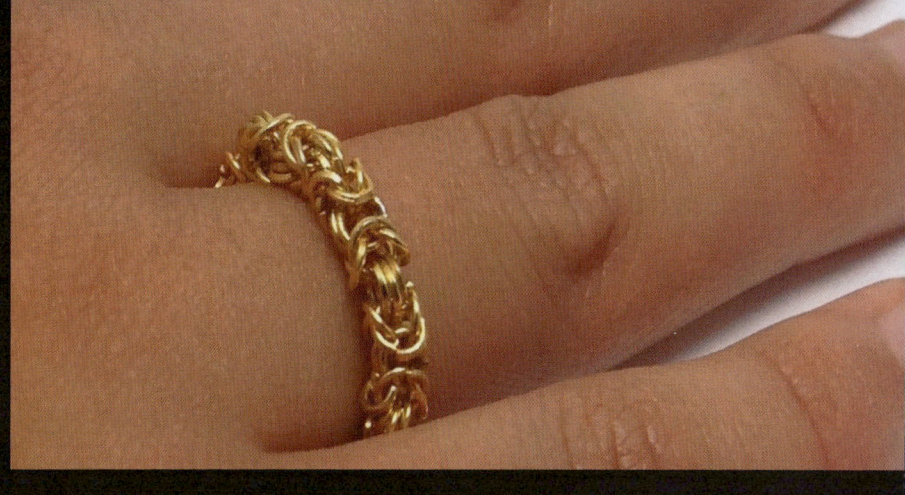

The repeating pattern of this ring is the perfect representation of never-ending love and friendship. Crafted in gold-plated jump rings.

TO CREATE YOU WILL NEED

126 Gold plated jump rings - 1.68mm ID, 24 gauge   Chain nose pliers
A piece of wire   Flat nose pliers

STEPS TO FOLLOW

STEP ONE

Using 123 gold plated jump rings, weave your chain following a 2-2-3 pattern instead of the usual 2-2-2 pattern. To be able to do this, link two jump rings to a pair of jump rings then attach three jump rings (figure 1). Take another two jump rings and link it to the three jump rings. Link two more jump rings to the pair of jump rings just attached (figure 2). Flip the last two jump rings like in steps two-three on page 22 then link three jump rings (figure 3). Repeat the pattern (figure 2 and 3) until you have reached your desired length. End your chain with four jump rings, a pair each like the way the chain started.

STEP TWO

Let the two ends meet together and link it to the remaining three jump rings. To do this, take the first end of the chain and flip the last pair of jump rings like in steps two-three on page 22. Attach an open jump ring and before closing the jump ring, take the other end of the chain and again flip the last pair of jump rings and continue linking the open jump ring. Close the ring. Triple the ring.

SQUARE RINGS DANGLY EARRINGS

A 4.8 inch colourful and sparkling pair of dangly earrings fashioned in an alternate square gold-plated triple byzantine weave and beautiful Swarovski elements square ring crystals secured with kidney ear wires.

TO CREATE YOU WILL NEED

224 medium gold plated jump rings - 2.65mm ID, 20 gauge
24 large gold plated jump rings - 6.88mm ID, 20 gauge
4 small gold plated jump rings - 1.68mm ID, 24 gauge
6 square rings Swarovski elements crystal beads
(2 tabac, 2 golden shade, 2 silver shade)

2 ear wire hooks
Chain nose pliers
Flat nose pliers

STEPS TO FOLLOW

STEP ONE

Using 53 medium gold plated jump rings (2.65mm ID, 20 gauge), create a chain in a triple link byzantine weave like in page 36 (figure 1). Once you've finished the chain, flip both ends like in page 22 step two (figure 2).

STEP TWO

Take your one open large jump ring (6.88mm ID, 20 gauge) and connect it to the weaved top four pairs of jump rings (figures 1-4), close the ring.

STEP THREE

Link the three remaining jump rings on both ends (figures 1-5). Make another component following steps one to three.

STEP FOUR

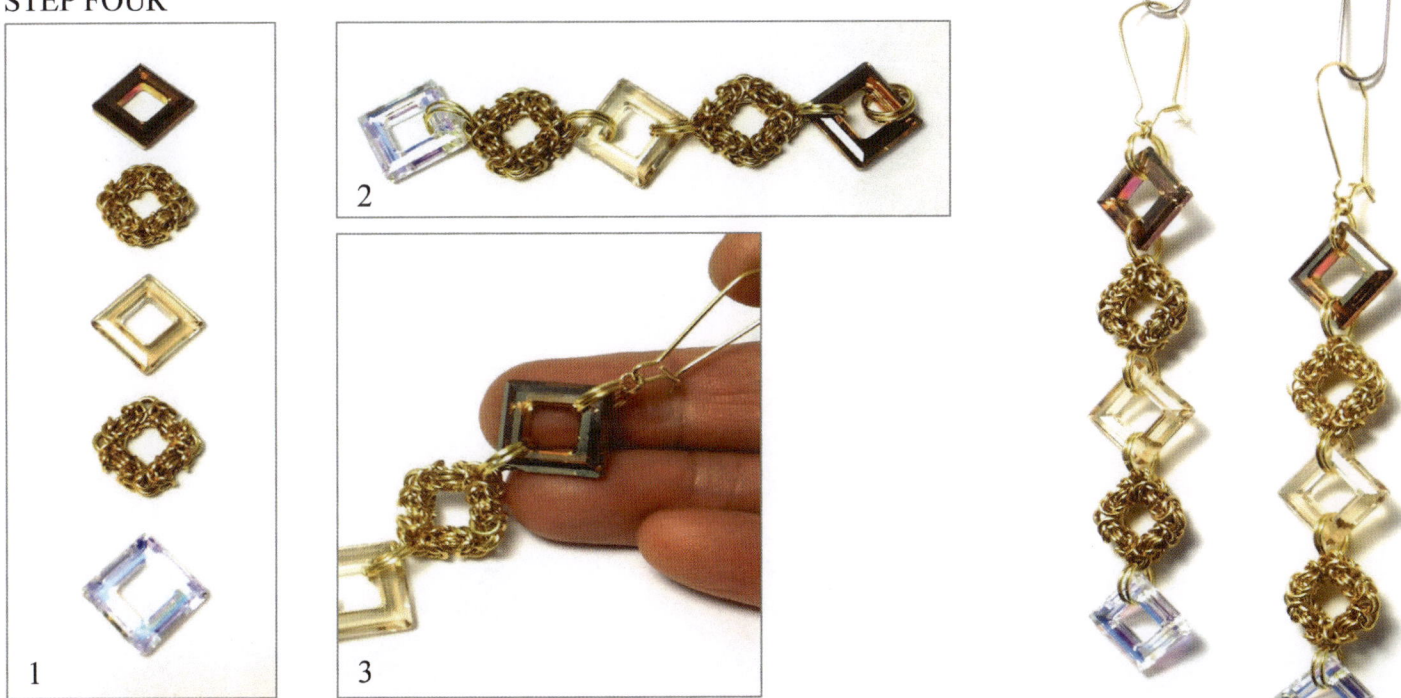

Take your two weaved components and three square Swarovski elements crystal beads. Lay them as for how you like them arranged. Connect all the pieces with two large gold plated jump rings (6.88mm ID, 20 gauge). Connect the last pair of jump rings at the top end of your crystal then link two small jump rings (1.68mm ID, 24 gauge) to these two and the ear wire hook. Repeat steps one-four to create the other pair.

BYZANTINE EARRINGS
DESIGN VARIATION

DIAMOND BYZANTINE
EARRINGS
(2.85")

BEADED DIAMOND
BYZANTINE EARRINGS
(2.25")

Two beautiful pairs of antique silver dangly
earrings that are displaying a diamond shape
design. One pair embellished with red round
coral beads. Perfect for any occasion.

TO CREATE YOU WILL NEED

Chain nose pliers, Round nose pliers, Flat nose pliers, Side cutters

For Beaded Diamond Byzantine Earrings

248 silver plated jump rings 2.53mm ID, 21 gauge
4 silver plated jump rings 5.79mm ID, 22 gauge
2 red coral beads 3.70mm
2 silver plated eye pins

For Diamond Byzantine Earrings

254 silver plated jump rings 3.45mm ID, 20 gauge
4 silver plated jump rings 5.58mm ID, 20 gauge
2 sterling silver ear wire hooks

STEPS TO FOLLOW

STEP ONE

Create a chain following steps one-seven on pages 22 and 23. Use 96 jump rings (3.45mm ID, 20 gauge) for Diamond Byzantine Earrings and (2.53mm ID, 21 gauge) for Beaded Diamond Byzantine Earrings.

STEP TWO

Connect both ends of your chain. To do this, flip back the last pair of jump rings on both ends of chain and link two jump rings.

STEP THREE

Once your chain is connected, arrange it into a square shape, and you can see the top end and bottom end corners of your square. Connect two pairs of jump ring on each corner. Notice a 2-2-2 chain (figure 1). Weave this chain like in steps two-four on page 22 (figure 2).

STEP FOUR

Fold back the four weaved chains as you twist the main chain ensuring that they are now inside the square. Take one jump ring (5.58mm ID, 20 gauge) for Beaded Diamond Byzantine Earrings and (5.79mm ID, 20 gauge) for Diamond Byzantine Earrings and pass it through each pair of jump rings. Double the ring.

STEP FIVE

For Diamond Byzantine Earrings, Arrange your earring into a diamond shape. Attach two jump rings at the top end, then take two more jump rings and connect it to the rings just attached and to the loop of the ear wire hook (figures 1-2). Finish your earring by attaching three jump rings at its bottom end (figure 3).

For Beaded Diamond Byzantine Earrings, thread your round coral bead into an eye pin and create another loop at the end of the bead to secure it (see page 16). Create a space where you are going to attach your bead by merely sliding apart the top and bottom two weaved chains at the centre of the diamond. Open the first loop of your bead and connect it to the two jump rings (5.79mm ID, 22 gauge) attached in the middle of your component. Close the loop. Repeat it to the opposite side. See figure 3. Next, link two jump rings at the top end of the earring then take one jump ring and attach it to the ear wire loop and the two jump rings just attached. See figures 4-6.

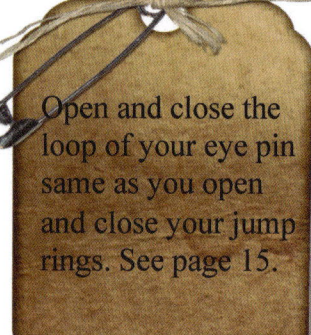

Open and close the loop of your eye pin same as you open and close your jump rings. See page 15.

chapter three

EUROPEAN 4 IN 1 WEAVE

The most common pattern in chain maille where each ring has four others linked to it.

This flat maille weave of Celtic inspiration can bring many designs into your jewellery making. Its flexibility and strength are obtained by connecting the rings to one another in interlocking fashion.

Experiment designs using these weave using different sizes and colours of jump rings and you'll be surprised what stunning pieces of jewellery you'll come up with it.

STEPS TO FOLLOW

STEP ONE

Scoop 4 jump rings with one open jump ring. Close your jump ring. Arrange your rings as shown in figure 4.

STEP TWO

Take an open jump ring and scoop two jump rings. Attach it to the last two jump rings from the right end (figure 2). Close your jump ring. It's best to lift your rings up with your pliers to be able to close the jump ring. Arrange your rings.

STEP THREE

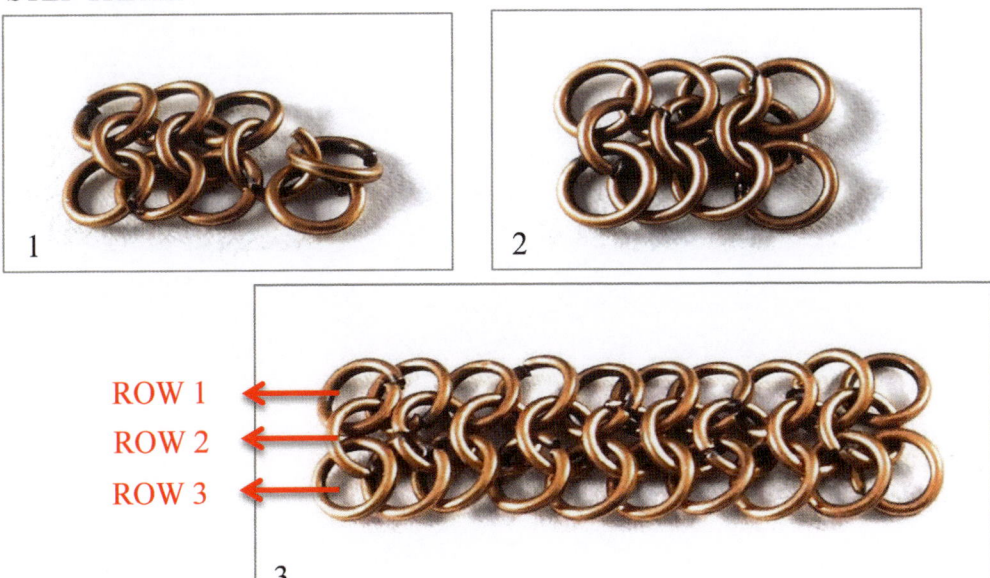

ROW 1
ROW 2
ROW 3

Continue weaving repeating step two until you have achieved your desired length. Make sure to arrange your woven rings before adding more jump rings as this will give you a more unobstructed view of your weave pattern. You'll also notice that your weave consists of three rows. See figure 3.

STEP FOUR

1 2

To continue adding rows, take one open jump ring and scoop two closed jump rings and connect it to the 1st and 2nd jump rings on the 3rd row of your weave. Arrange your rings. You now have five rows.

STEP FIVE

From now on, just scoop **one** closed jump ring with one open jump ring and pass it through the 2nd jump ring on the 5th row, then connect it to the 2nd and 3rd jump rings on the 3rd row of your weave. Arrange your rings. Repeat step five to continue with your pattern until you reach the end of the row, keeping in mind where to connect the rings. Continue adding rows until you've reached your desired width.

EUROPEAN 4 IN 1 CHAIN COLLAR

This 18-inch simple collar weaved in triple rows of silver plated jump rings is ideal for everyday elegance and a stunning wear for any style of occasion. Finished with a stylish sterling silver J-hook and eye clasp.

TO CREATE YOU WILL NEED

213 silver plated jump rings - 5.34mm ID, 17 gauge
Sterling silver hook and eye clasp - 23.96mm long x 10.18mm wide

Chain nose pliers
Flat nose pliers

STEPS TO FOLLOW

STEP ONE

Before you start, open 73 jump rings and leave the 140 jump rings closed. Set aside four open jump rings. Create your chain. Follow European 4 in 1 weave steps one-three on pages 44-45 until you have reached the length of this collar.

STEP TWO

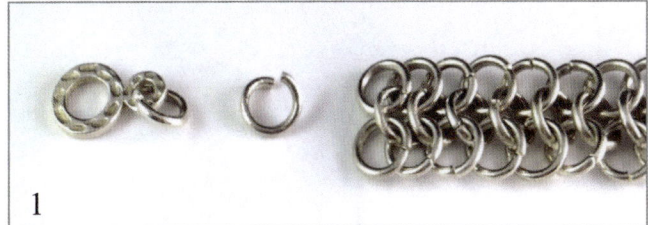

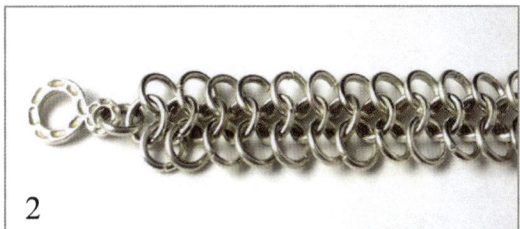

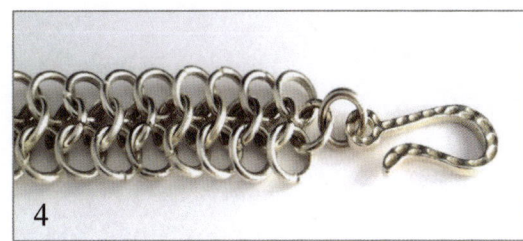

Attach one jump ring to the loop of your clasp (figure 1). Take another jump ring and attach it to one end of your collar and the jump ring just attached (figure 2). Repeat the same step for the other end of your collar (figures 3 and 4).

INVERTED TRIANGLE COLLAR

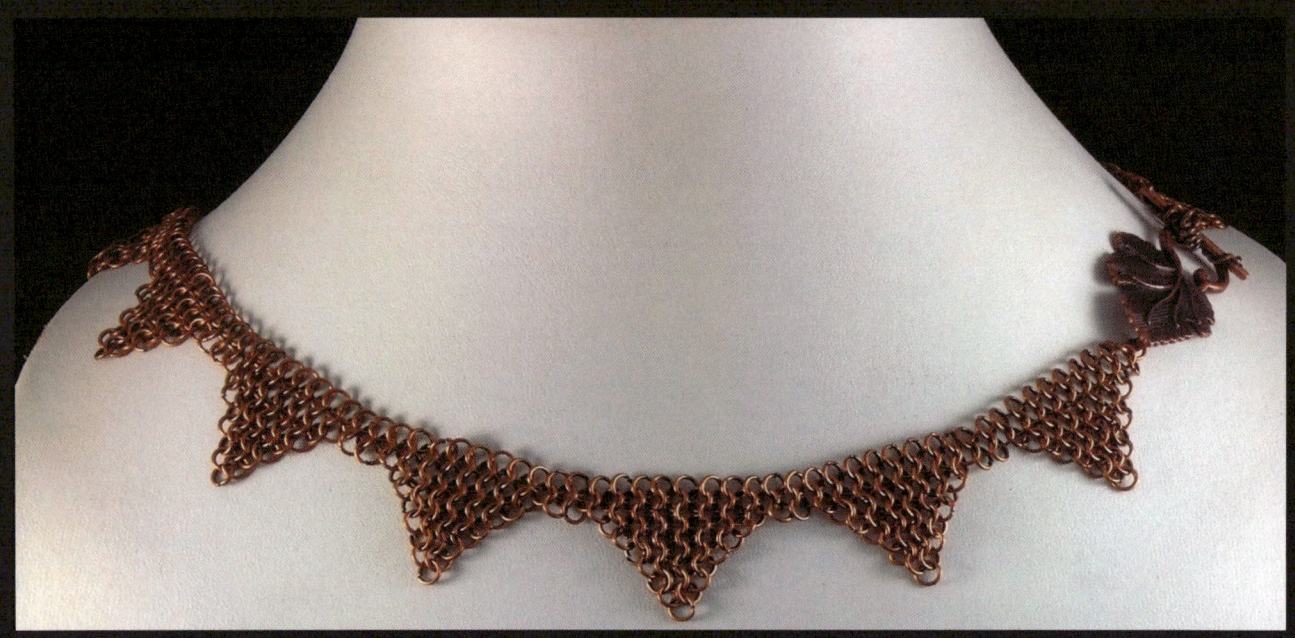

This classic and fashionable collar can be worn showing either front, back or sideways for versatility. It is 20 inches in length and finished with a grape leaf toggle clasp which accentuates the beauty of the design.

TO CREATE YOU WILL NEED

813 antique copper jump rings - 2.79mm ID, 22 gauge
1 antique copper grape leaf toggle clasp
Chain nose pliers
Long nose pliers

1. Before you start, prepare your 533 open jump rings and 280 closed jump rings. This will make the flow of your work continuously.
2. Each inverted triangle needs 57 jump rings (20 closed jump rings and 37 open jump rings).
3. Weave your 14 inverted triangles first before connecting them together.

STEPS TO FOLLOW

PHASE I - WEAVE 14 INVERTED TRIANGLES

STEP ONE

Weave three rows of jump rings following the European 4 in 1 weave on pages 44 and 45. Your first row will have ten jump rings, second row with nine jump rings and third row with ten jump rings. Your weave should look like above.

STEP TWO

Prepare your seven open jump rings to be attached to the next row.

STEP THREE

Connect one ring at a time. Starting from the 2nd ring on the 3rd row, attach an open jump ring and pass it through the 3rd jump ring. Close jump ring.

STEP FOUR

Take another open jump ring. Attach it to the 3rd jump ring and pass it through the 4th jump ring. Close jump ring.

49

STEP FIVE

Continue attaching an open jump ring from 4th ring to 5th ring, 5th ring to 6th ring, 6th ring to 7th ring, 7th ring to 8th ring, and 8th ring to 9th ring. Leaving the 10th ring unattached. The result should be the same as photo shown above.

STEP SIX

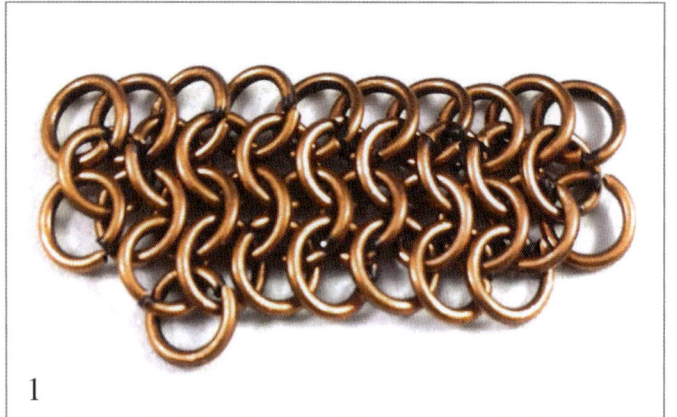

1

2

3

4

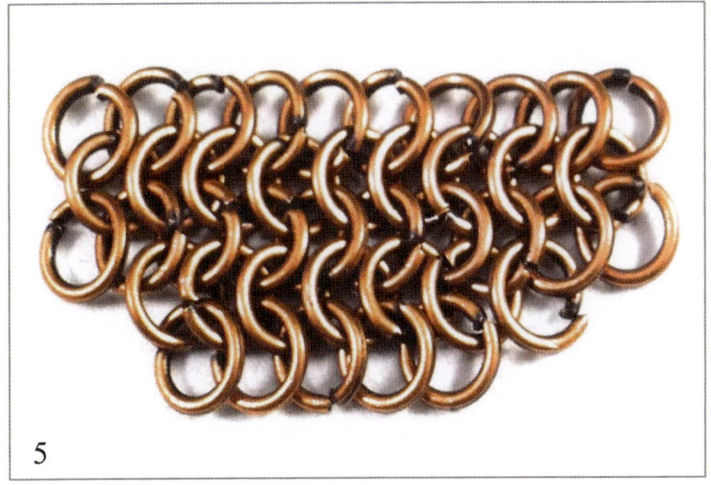

5

6

For your next row, you have to connect 6 open jump rings to the previously attached rings one at a time. Attach an open ring to the 1st ring and pass it through to the 2nd ring. Close the ring. Continue attaching the 2nd and 3rd rings, 3rd and 4th rings, 4th and 5th rings, 5th and 6th rings, and 6th and 7th rings with an open jump ring. Close jump ring. See figures 1-6.

STEP SEVEN

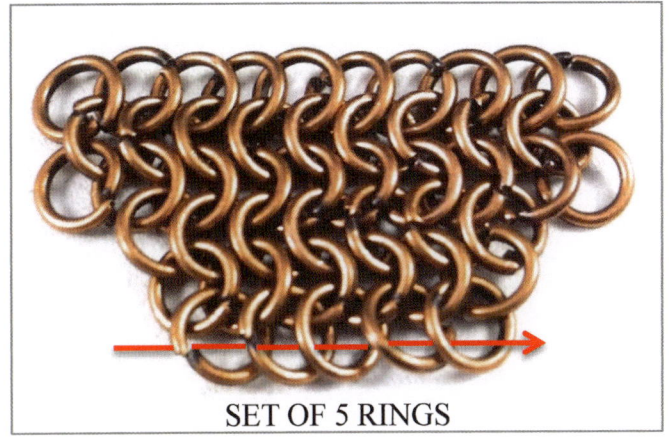

SET OF 5 RINGS

SET OF 4 RINGS

SET OF 3 RINGS

SET OF 2 RINGS

1 LAST RING

Carry on weaving by following step six with your set of 5 rings, then set of 4 rings, set of 3 rings, set of 2 rings, and your last one ring to make the final look of your inverted triangle. *You have now created your first inverted triangle. Continue making 13 more inverted triangles following the steps in Phase 1.*

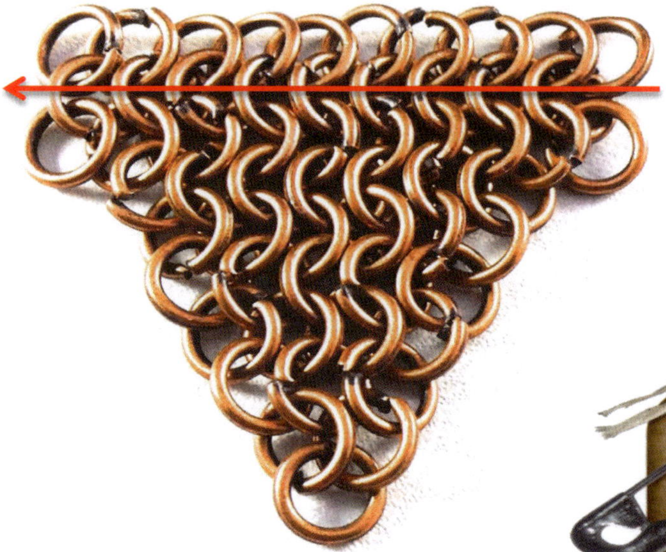

FIGURE 2

FIGURE 1

To weave your next inverted triangle, finish step 1 (figure 2). Then before continuing to the next step, lay your pattern down on a surface. Ensure that the middle section of figure 2 is going into the same direction as the middle section in the 1st inverted triangle weaved (figure 1). It is crucial to the design as you want all your inverted triangles to get connected in the same way.

PHASE II – CONNECT ALL 14 INVERTED TRIANGLES

STEP ONE

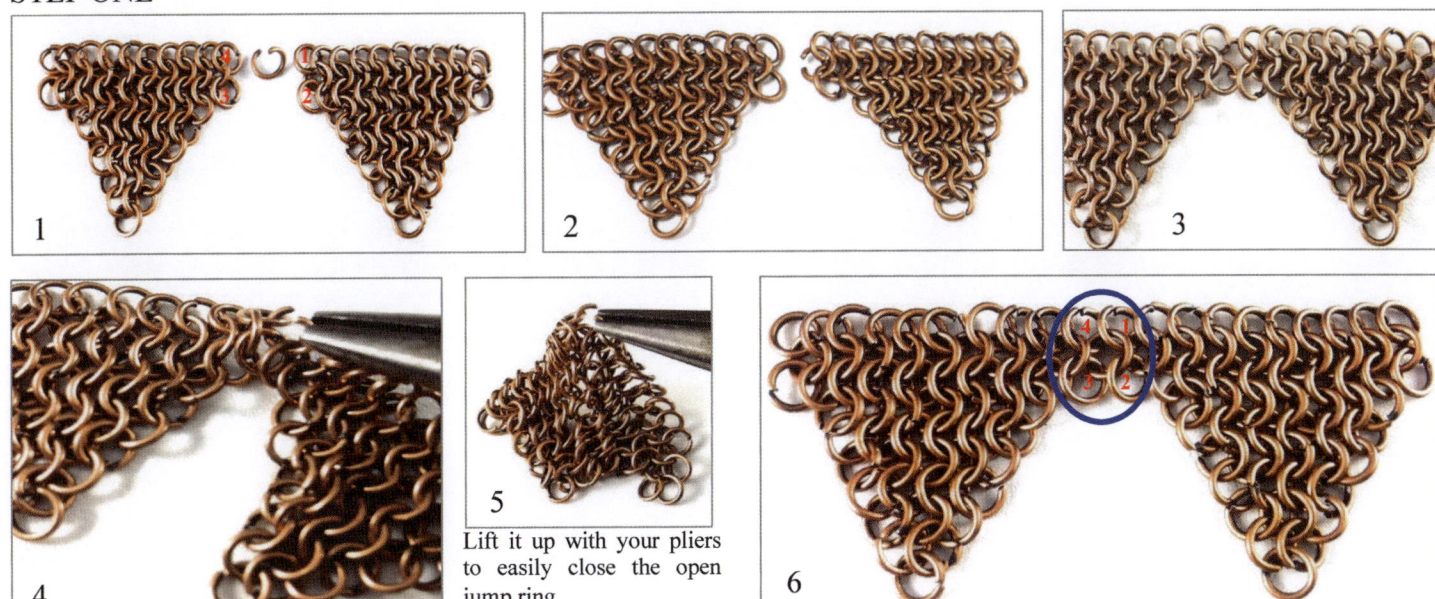

With one open jump ring connect two inverted triangles together. Pass the open jump ring to the 1st and 2nd ring then to the 3rd ring and out through to the 4th ring (figures1-4). Close jump ring. See figure 6. Continue connecting all the other inverted triangles.

PHASE III – FINISH WITH TOGGLE CLASP

STEP ONE

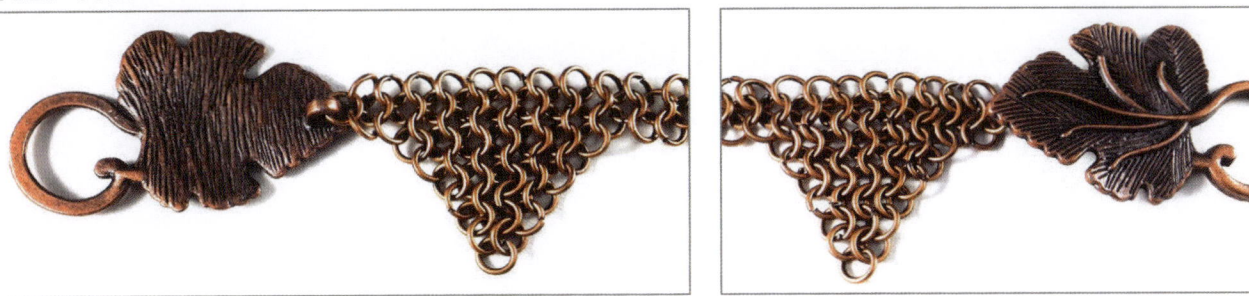

Simply connect one open jump ring to one end of your collar. Using the same open ring, connect it to the end of your toggle clasp. Close jump ring.

STEP TWO

Connect one open jump ring to the toggle bar. Close the ring. Take another open jump ring and connect it to the other end of your collar and to the ring just attached to the toggle bar. Close jump ring.

EUROPEAN 4 IN 1 JEWELLERY SET

CHOKER

A beautiful choker that sits smoothly around the neck in antique copper and gold plated jump rings. It's finished with a sizeable bold clasp that acts stunningly as a pendant and adds a touch of old-world elegance. Its final length including clasp is 16.6in/42.2cm.

TO CREATE YOU WILL NEED

1004 antique copper jump rings - 2.79mm ID, 21 gauge   Chain nose pliers
315 gold plated jump rings - 2.79mm ID, 21 gauge   Flat nose pliers
1 shell box clasp – 31.70mm x 35.23mm

STEPS TO FOLLOW

STEP ONE

Make 34 sets of these following the European 4 in 1 Weave on pages 44-45. A set is made up of 3 rows with ten pairs of copper jump rings connected by nine copper jump rings.

STEP TWO

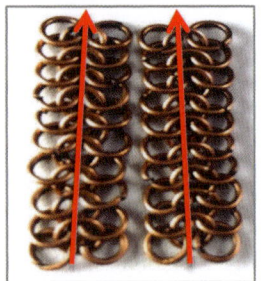 1   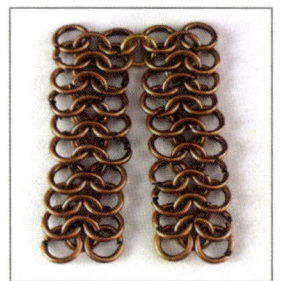 2    3

Pair your first two sets of weave making sure that the middle row of both sets is going in the same direction preferably the ascending path. See figure 1. Connect each set of weave with gold jump rings. See figures 2 and 3.

HOW TO CONNECT YOUR SET OF WEAVES

1. Starting from Set B, connect one gold open jump ring to the 1st copper jump ring and pass it through to the 2nd copper ring then attach it to the 2nd copper ring in Set A passing from the bottom and out through the 1st ring. Close your ring by lifting them up from the surface using your pliers. (Note: you can either start from Set A or B depending on which side you are most comfortable. In this step instructions, I've started with Set B to Set A).

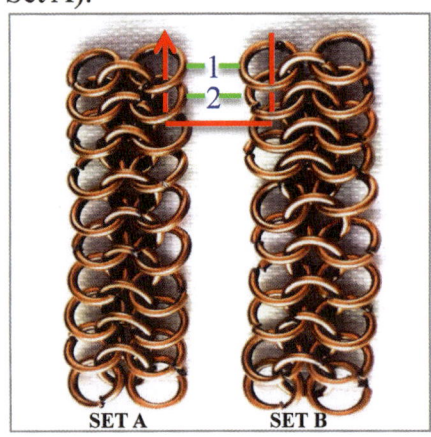      

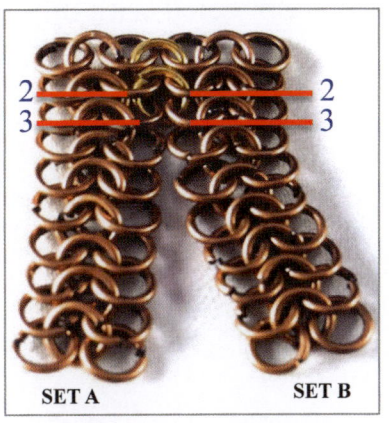

SET A   **SET B**

2. Starting from **Set B**, connect one gold open jump ring from the 2nd copper jump ring passing through to the 3rd copper jump ring then attach it to **Set A** on the 3rd copper jump ring coming from the bottom and out to the 2nd copper jump ring. Close your gold open jump ring by lifting them up with your pliers.

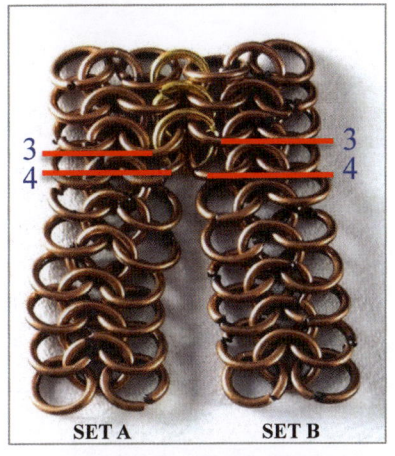

SET A   **SET B**

3. Connect the 3rd gold open ring to Set B from 3rd ring to 4th ring then to Set A from the 4th ring coming from the bottom and passing out through the 3rd ring. Close gold ring.

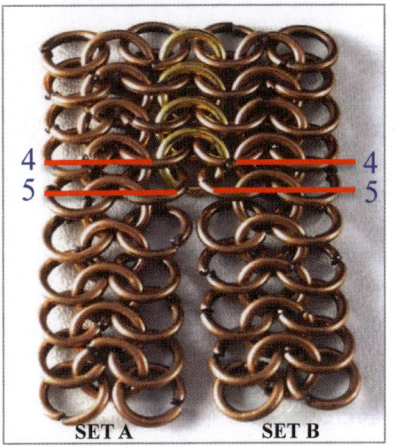

SET A   **SET B**

4. Connect the 4th gold open ring to Set B from 4th ring to 5th ring then to Set A from the 5th ring coming from the bottom and passing out through the 4th ring. Close gold ring.

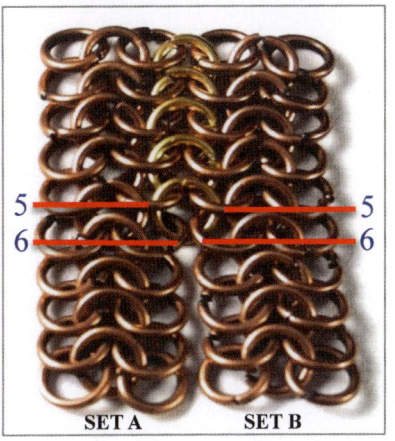

SET A   **SET B**

5. Connect the 5th gold open ring to Set B from 5th ring to 6th ring then to Set A from the 6th ring coming from the bottom and passing out through the 5th ring. Close gold ring.

6. Continue connecting an open gold jump ring from Set B rings to Set A rings following the same procedure as the previous steps until your two sets of weave are connected with nine gold rings.

| SET A | SET B | | SET A | SET B | | SET A | SET B | | SET A | SET B |

STEP THREE

Connect all 34 sets of weave and then attach nine gold rings at each end of the pattern.

STEP FOUR

Connect your clasp. Attach one open copper jump ring to the first three top gold rings then attach it to the first ring attached to the clasp. Close jump ring. Double the jump ring. See figures 1 and 2.

STEP FIVE

Attach another copper jump ring to the three middle gold rings then attach it to the second ring attached to the clasp. Close ring. Double the ring.

STEP SIX

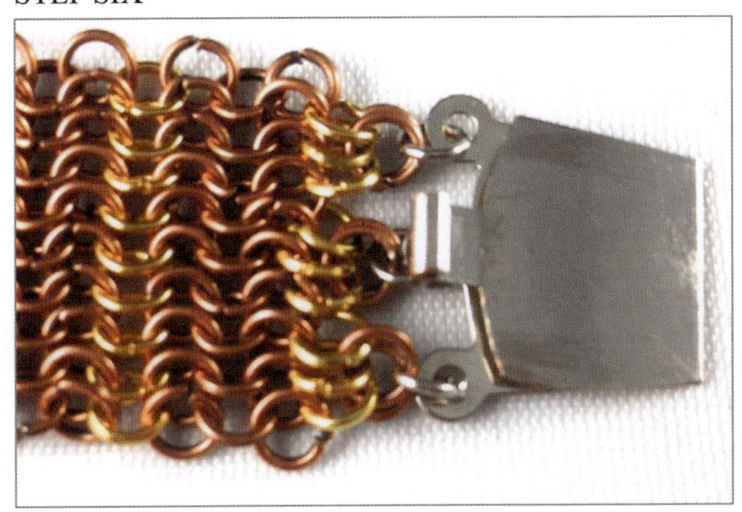

Attach the last bottom three gold rings with an open copper jump ring then connect it to the third ring attached to the clasp. Close ring. Double the ring.

STEP SEVEN

Take the other clasp, connect two copper jump rings in each loop. Repeat steps four-six.

NECKLACE

This antique copper and golden beauty weaved together row by row is a warm and sensual necklace and showcases delicate and intricate work. Finished with gold plated lobster clasp and it's 19.2 inches in total length.

TO CREATE YOU WILL NEED

486 antique copper jump rings - 2.79mm ID, 22 gauge
127 gold plated jump rings - 2.79mm ID, 22 gauge
2 gold plated jump rings - 4.10mm ID, 19 gauge
1 gold plated lobster clasp (7.30mm wide x 13.86mm long)
Chain nose pliers
Flat nose pliers

1. For a faster and continuous work flow, open jump rings first before you start your weave.
2. Open 134 copper jump rings and 47 gold plated jump rings. Leave the rest of the jump rings closed.

STEPS TO FOLLOW

STEP ONE

Make 6 sets

Connect these sets with nine gold jump rings

Create your pendant. To do this, weave three rows of copper jump rings using the European 4 in 1 weave. Create six sets of these. A set is made of three rows with ten pairs of copper jump rings connected by nine copper jump rings. Connect these six sets using gold jump rings. See step two on pages 56-58 on how to connect your weaves.

STEP TWO

Create your chain. To do this, scoop two closed copper jump rings with an open copper jump ring and link it to the first two jump rings at the right end of your pendant. Close the ring.

STEP THREE

Before you continue adding your chain, connect one gold open jump ring to the 10th copper ring from 5th row passing through the 10th ring and 11th ring from the 3rd row. Close gold ring. This ring gives an added support for the pendant when it's hanged on the neck.

STEP FOUR

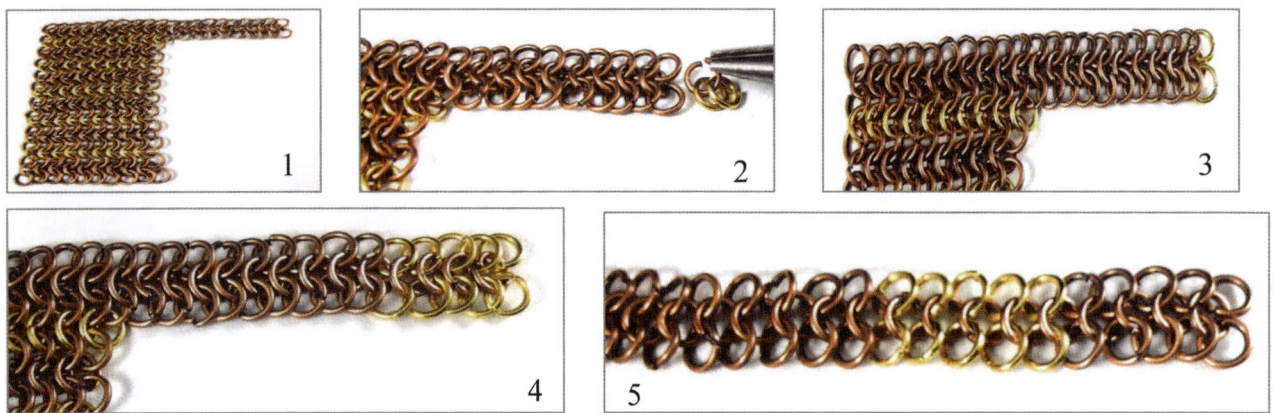

Continue adding your chain till you have attached ten pairs of copper jump rings connected by nine copper jump rings. This time, attach five pairs of gold jump rings connected by four copper jump rings. Alternate the colours with ten pairs of copper rings then five pairs of gold rings till you've reached the desired length. End your chain with five pairs of copper jump rings. Repeat steps one-three to make the other end of your chain.

STEP FIVE

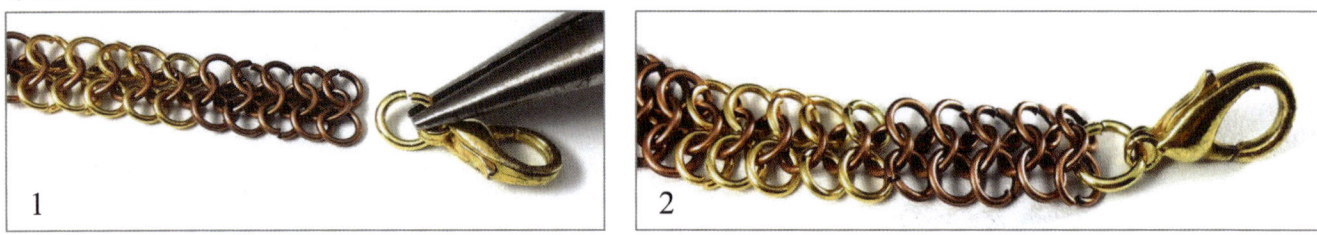

Attach your lobster clasp. To do this, Take one open gold plated jump ring (4.10mm ID, 19 gauge) and attach it to the lobster clasp's loop then to one end of your chain. Close the gold plated jump ring. See figure 2.

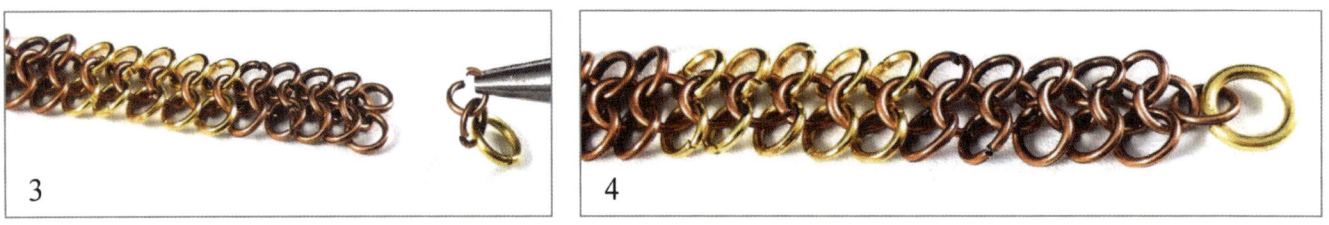

Next, attach one gold plated jump ring (4.10mm ID, 19 gauge) to the other end of the chain. To do this, take one open copper jump ring and connect it to the gold jump ring. Close the ring. Take another open copper jump ring and link it to the previously attached copper jump ring and to the other end of chain. Close the ring.

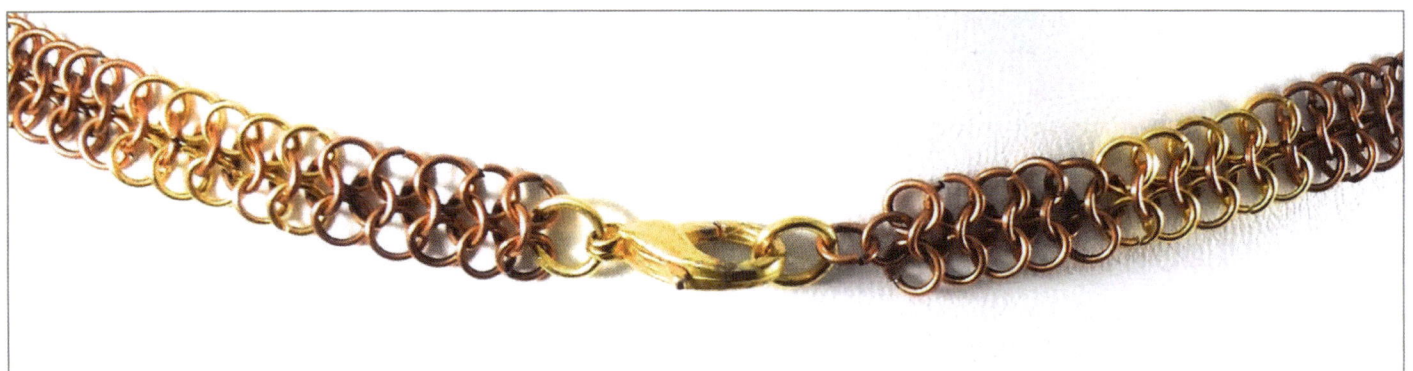

DANGLY EARRINGS

These beautiful dangly earrings give an air of old world charm and sophistication. These are sets of antique copper jump rings weaved row by row and connected by gold plated jump rings for extra colour and style. A 2.75 inches long and finished with gold-plated ear wire hooks.

TO CREATE YOU WILL NEED

140 antique copper jump rings - 2.79mm ID, 22 gauge
34 gold plated jump rings - 2.79mm ID, 22 gauge
2 gold plated ear wires

Chain nose pliers
Flat nose pliers

STEPS TO FOLLOW

STEP ONE

Create three rows of European 4 in 1 weave using copper jump rings. See steps one-three on pages 44-45. The rows consist of five jump rings, and four jump rings alternately. Make five sets of these then link each set with four gold jump rings (see pages 56-58 on how to connect your sets of weaves).

STEP TWO

1   2   3

Take one gold open jump ring then attach it to your ear wire (figure 1) and to the five copper jump rings at the end of your weave (figure 2). Close gold jump ring (figure 3). Finish the other pair.

STEP THREE

Repeat steps one and two to make the other pair

FLORETS CHAIN COLLAR

This earthy toned floral style collar can be worn with a sophisticated updo or a messy ponytail. It's 17 inches in total length including clasp. Finished securely with a grape leaf toggle clasp.

TO CREATE YOU WILL NEED

548 antique copper jump rings 2.79mm ID, 22 gauge
1 antique grape leaf toggle clasp

Chain nose pliers
Flat nose pliers

STEPS TO FOLLOW

STEP ONE

Create your chain with European 4 in 1 weave.
See pages 44-45. Create a chain of three rows.
(1st row has 156 rings, 2nd row has 155 rings,
and 3rd row has 156 rings).

STEP TWO

Starting from the bottom right end of your chain, scoop four jump rings with an open jump ring.
See figure 1. Close jump ring. See figure 2. Repeat on the opposite row. See figure 3.

STEP THREE

Repeat step two until you have scooped all the rings
in the chain. And now, you have a chain of florets.

STEP FOUR

Finish your collar by adding your closures. Take the first end of your chain and open the ring attached. Connect it to the end of your toggle clasp and close the jump ring. Connect three rings one at a time at the second end of your chain and before you close the last ring, attach it to the toggle bar.

STAR PENDANT CHOKER

A stunning star design pendant beautifully woven in an antique bronze jump rings hung from this graceful and elegant floral designed choker.

TO CREATE YOU WILL NEED

For the choker: 548 antique copper jump rings - 2.79mm ID, 22 gauge
            1 antique copper leaf toggle clasp

Chain nose pliers
Flat nose pliers

For the pendant: 54 antique copper jump rings (2.79mm ID, 22 gauge)

STEPS TO FOLLOW

STEP ONE

To create the choker, refer to pages 66-67. You can decide to make the length longer or shorter.

STEP TWO

For the pendant, weave fifteen pairs of jump rings connected by fourteen jump rings. Refer to European 4 in 1 weave on pages 44-45.

STEP THREE

Take one open jump ring and scoop three rings on your first bottom row of weave on the right. Close the ring. Double the ring by passing it through to the first ring just attached to form a Mobius knot. Then triple the ring by passing it through to the two previously attached rings.

ATTACHING THE 3 RINGS TO FORM A MOBIUS KNOT

STEP FOUR

Repeat step three until
you have weaved five sets
of florets from your first
row.

STEP FIVE

Flip your piece so that the knotted row is now on the left side. Open one gold plated jump ring and scoop all
the fifteen rings in the opposite row. Close your ring.

STEP SIX

 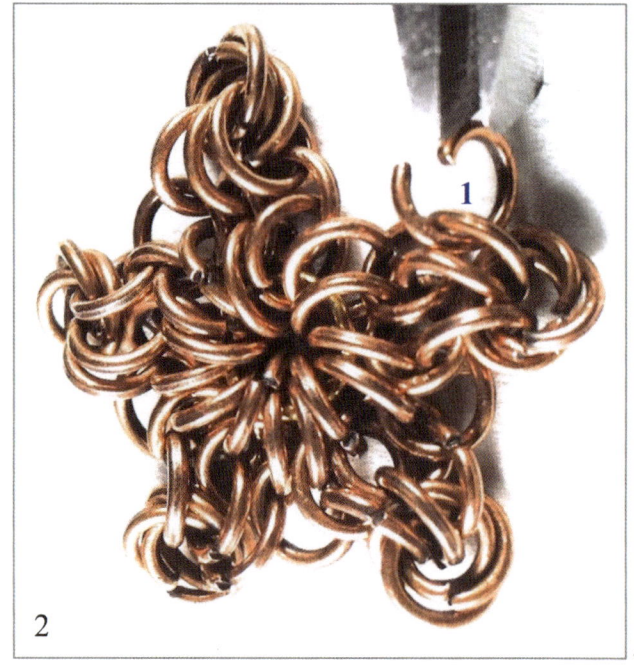

70

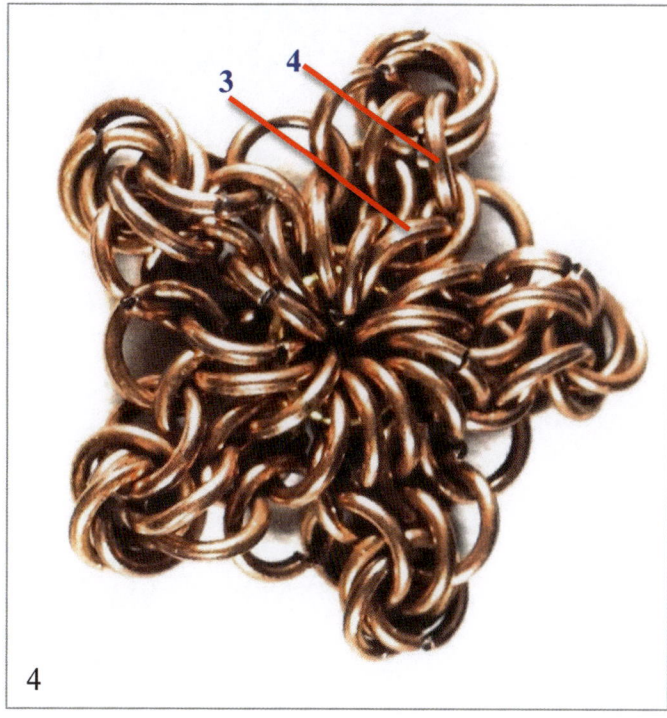

To finally form the star pendant, you need one copper jump ring to connect the four copper jump rings. To do this, pass your open jump ring through the first ring and passing it through the second ring (figure 3). While scooping the two rings together, move it closer to be able to connect it to the third ring and passing it through to the fourth ring. Close the ring (figure 4).

STEP SEVEN

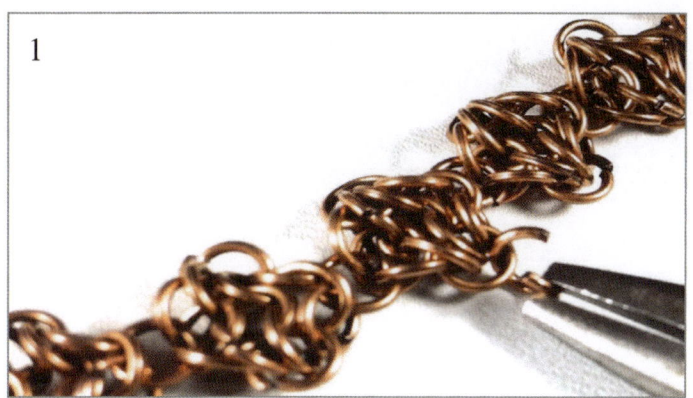

Connect one open jump ring to your choker and to the star pendant. Close the ring.

SUNFLOWER PENDANT CHOKER

Suspended from this elegant and graceful floral choker is a carefully woven sunflower design pendant made from antique bronze micro jump rings.

TO CREATE YOU WILL NEED

For the choker: 548 antique copper jump rings - 2.79mm ID, 22 gauge
                1 antique copper leaf toggle clasp

Chain nose pliers
Flat nose pliers

For the pendant: 134 antique copper jump rings - 2.79mm ID, 22 gauge

STEPS TO FOLLOW

STEP ONE

To make your choker, refer to pages 66-67.

STEP TWO

To make the sunflower pendant, weave your chain in three rows consisting of 32 pairs of jump ring connected by 31 jump rings using the European 4 in 1 weave pattern. See pages 44-45.

STEP THREE

Next, make your florets. To do this, take one open jump ring and scoop the first four jump rings from the bottom row of your chain. Close the ring. Double the ring by going through it forming a knot.

STEP FOUR

Repeat step three to the opposite row of the chain. You now have formed one floret. Repeat steps three and four for the remaining rings till you have created your eight florets

STEP FIVE

1

2

3

4

Pair the florets on the right end. To do this, take one open jump ring and attach the two knots together. Close the ring. Continue pairing the remaining six florets with one jump ring.

STEP SIX

1

2

3

Take one open jump ring to connect the four rings that just paired the florets in step five. Close the ring. Double the ring.

STEP SEVEN

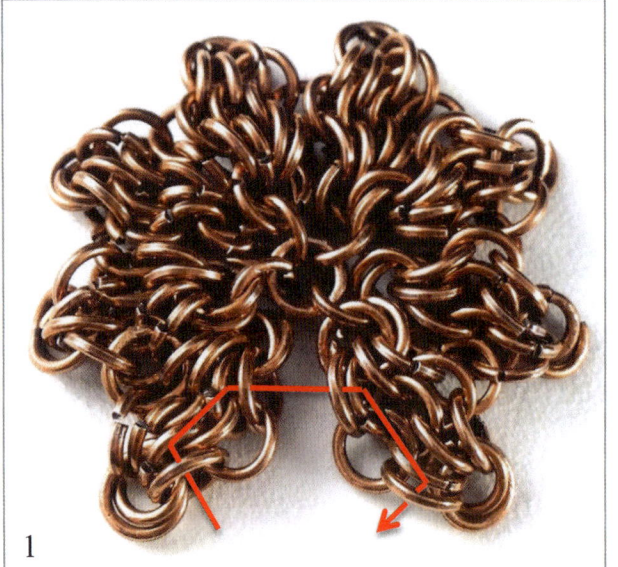

1

2

3

4

Your sunflower pendant is now in form and we just need to connect the rings together. With one open jump ring, connect the gap by attaching 1st and 2nd jump ring on the left end of the pendant then connect it through the 3rd ring coming from the bottom then pass it through the 4th jump ring on the right end of the pendant. Close the ring.

STEP EIGHT

You can now attach your sunflower pendant to your choker. Take one open jump ring, attach the ring to one of the knots of your pendant then connect it to the middle part of the choker. Close the ring.

KNOTTED EUROPEAN
4 IN 1
DROP EARRINGS

A 2 inch simple and elegant pair of drop earrings fashioned from silver plated jump rings, set with rich ruby Swarovski elements crystal and finished with stylish hoop ear studs with ear backs.

TO CREATE YOU WILL NEED

30 silver plated jump rings - 5.34mm ID, 17 gauge
2 silver plated jump rings - 4.92mm ID, 23 gauge
2 ruby Swarovski elements teardrop crystal beads
2 sterling silver ear studs with ear backs
Chain nose pliers
Flat nose pliers

STEPS TO FOLLOW

STEP ONE

 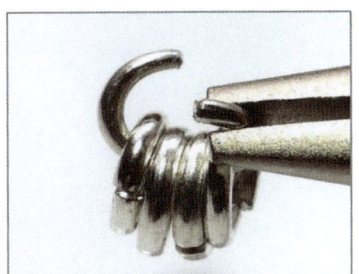 

Take one open jump ring with your chain nose plier. Scoop four closed jump rings. Close the open jump ring. Arrange your rings.

STEP TWO

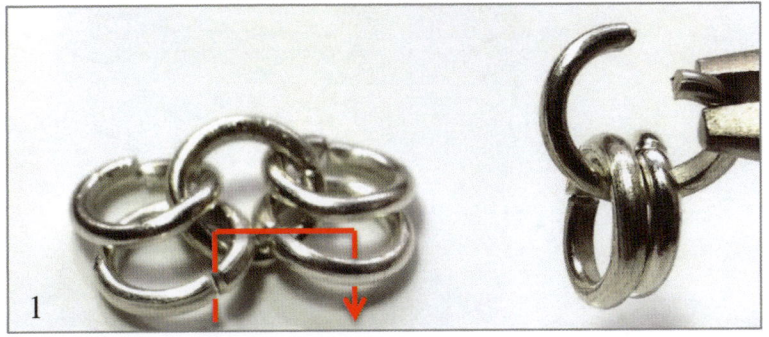 

Take one open ring with your chain nose plier. Scoop two closed jump rings and attach the open jump ring to the first two rings previously attached in step one. Close the ring. Arrange your rings.

Play with different sizes and colours of jump rings and beads as well as ear wire hooks, and you'll come up with your fresh design.

77

STEP THREE

Take one open ring and attach it to the first two rings previously attached in step two. Close the ring. Form a knot as you double the jump ring by passing through it.

STEP FOUR

Take one open ring and attach it to your earring stud and the two rings previously knotted in step three. Close the ring.

STEP FIVE

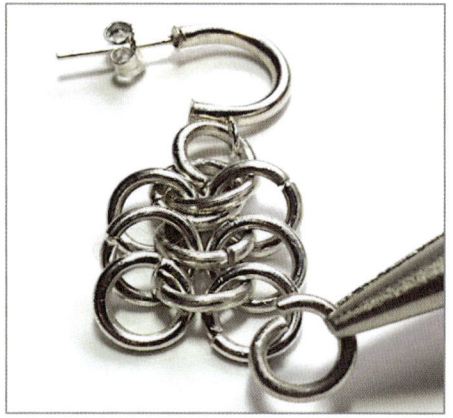  

Take one open jump ring and attach it to the three rings on the right side coming from the bottom right up through the top. Close the ring. Double the ring by going through it forming a knot.

STEP SIX

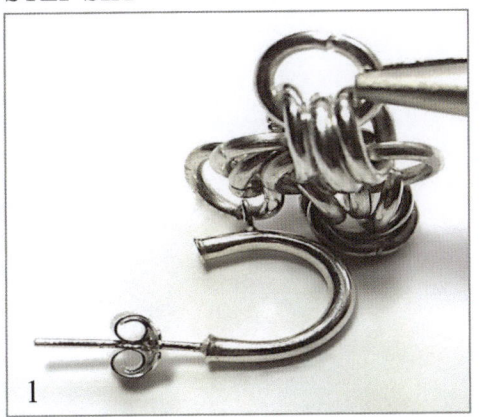

Repeat step five to the three rings on the left side. Your earrings should now look like in figure 3.

STEP SEVEN

Now take one open jump ring (4.92mm ID, 23 gauge) and attach it to your teardrop bead then attach it to the first two rings from the bottom. Close the ring. Repeat steps one-seven to create the other pair of your earring.

DIAMOND COPPER RING

A beautiful ring, displaying an intricate and magnificent diamond design. Fabulous for everyday wear.

TO CREATE YOU WILL NEED

128 antique copper jump rings - 2.79mm ID, 22 gauge
Chain nose pliers
Flat nose pliers

STEPS TO FOLLOW

STEP ONE

With one open jump ring, scoop two closed jump rings. Close jump ring. Arrange your jump rings. See figure 2. The jump ring at the top will be your first row. The two jump rings at the bottom will be your second row.

STEP TWO

Create your third row. Link three jump rings to the two jump ring attached in step one. Take one open jump ring and attach it to the second jump ring on the right. Close jump ring. Take another open jump ring and pass it through to the 1st jump ring on the left then through to the 2nd ring on the right. Close jump ring. Take your last open jump ring and connect it to the 1st jump ring on the left. Close jump ring. Your pattern should now look like in figure 3.

STEP THREE

Create your fourth row by linking four jump rings to the three jump rings attached in step two. Attach an open jump ring to the third jump ring on the right then close jump ring. Take the 2nd open jump ring, pass it through to the second jump ring then pass it through to the third jump ring. Close jump ring. Take the 3rd open jump ring and pass it through to the first then through to the second jump ring. Close jump ring. Take the 4th jump ring and link it to the first jump ring. Close jump ring.

STEP FOUR

Continue creating your rows until you have reached the 10th row. You have now finished the half of your diamond ring.

STEP FIVE

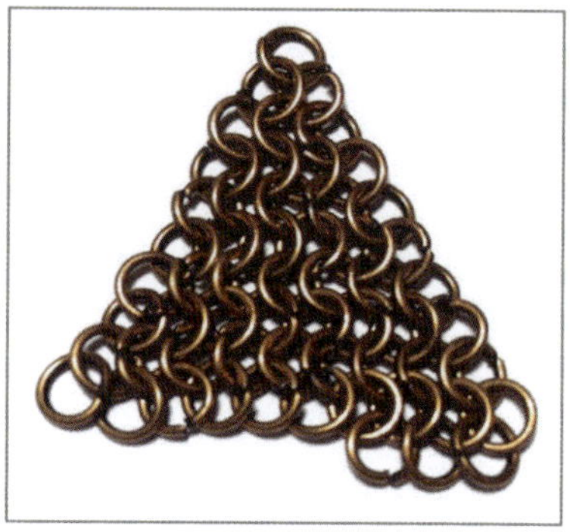

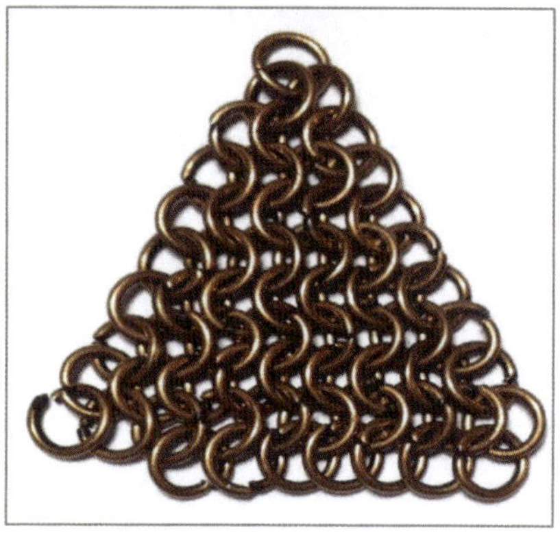

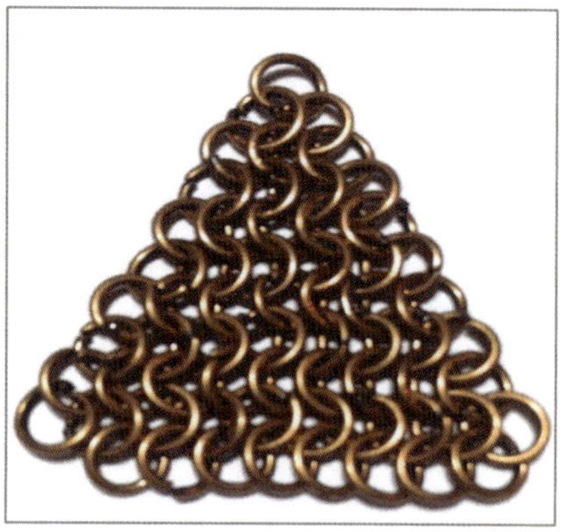

Create the other half of your diamond ring. This time, create your first row by linking nine jump rings to the 10th row of the first half of your diamond. Attach your second row by connecting eight rings. Continue until you have connected all the rows down to the last row with one jump ring.

STEP SIX

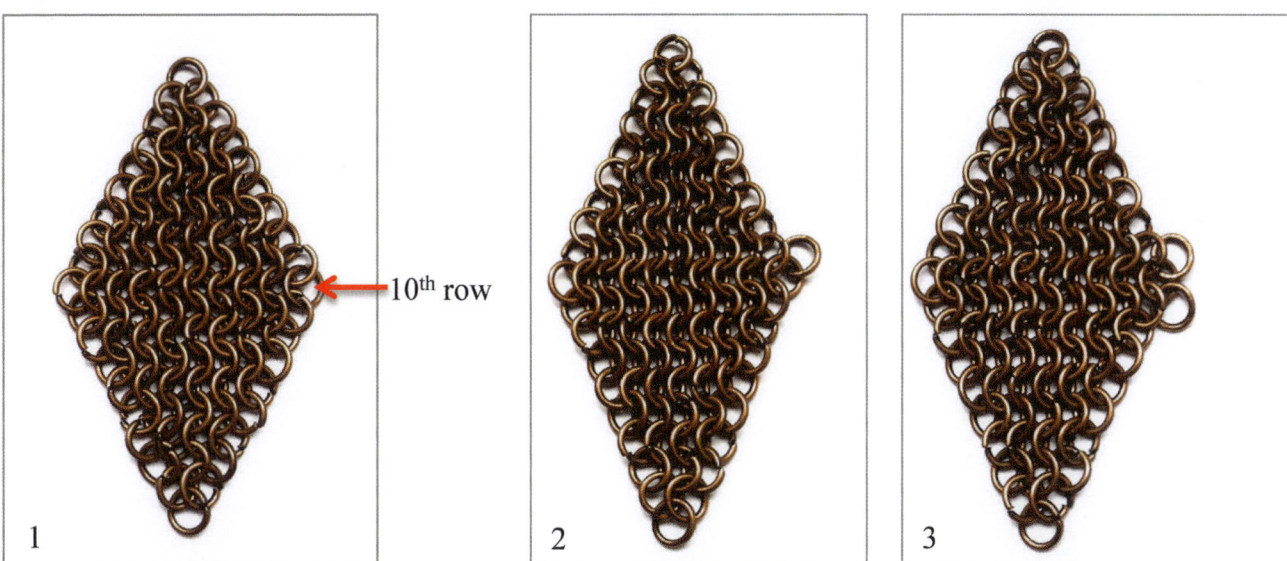

10th row

At the tenth row of your diamond, where the two halves of your diamond meet, connect two jump rings. Take an open jump ring and attach it to the first jump ring on the right of the tenth row. Close jump ring. Connect another jump ring. Arrange your rings as shown in figure 3.

STEP SEVEN

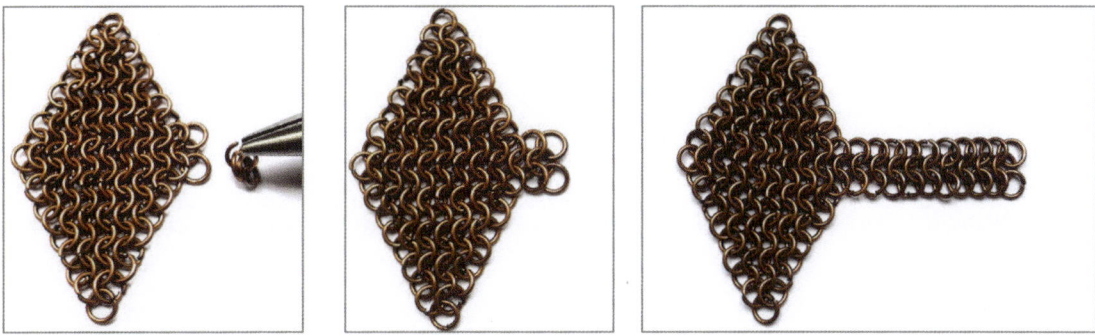

To continue with the length of your chain, scoop two closed jump rings with one open jump ring then connect it to the two jump rings just attached in step six (See step two on page 44). Continue until you have created the desired length.

STEP EIGHT

To connect your ring, open the first jump ring from the 10th row of your diamond at the other end, then link it to the two jump rings at the end of the chain. Close jump ring.

KNOTTED EUROPEAN 4 IN 1 HEART BRACELET

A captivating silver plated knotted European 4 in 1 Bracelet. Stylish and beautiful, this segmented bracelet is perfect for most everyday outfits or a perfect pair to a black dress. Finished with a secure heart lobster clasp and 7 1/2 inches in length with an added extender for that extra length.

TO CREATE YOU WILL NEED

178 silver plated jump rings - 5.34mm ID, 17 gauge
1 silver plated heart lobster clasp
Flat nose plier
Chain nose plier

STEPS TO FOLLOW

STEP ONE

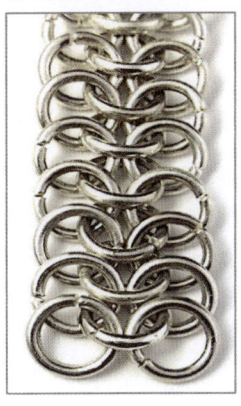

Create a chain following a European 4 in 1 weave. See pages 44 and 45. Your chain should consist of 36 jump rings on first row, 35 jump rings on second row and 36 jump rings on the third row.

STEP TWO

1

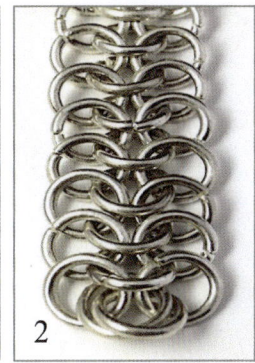

2

At the end of the chain attach an open jump ring. Close jump ring (figure1). Take another open jump ring and pass it through to the ring just attached to form a knot. Close the ring (figure 2).

STEP THREE

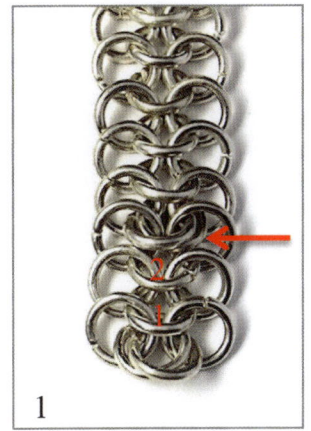

1

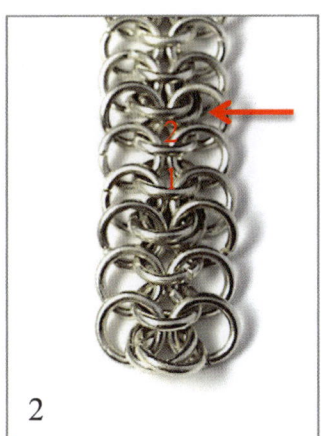

2

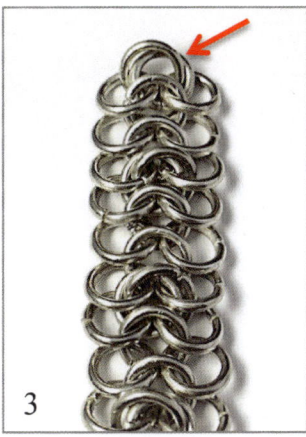

3

Looking at the middle row, skip two jump rings after the two knotted rings in step two then attach one open jump ring to double the next ring. Form a knot by passing through it before closing the ring (figure 1). Repeat this step until you have done it to the whole chain (figure 3). At the end of the chain, attach one ring and form a knot as you double the ring like in step two.

STEP FOUR

1

2

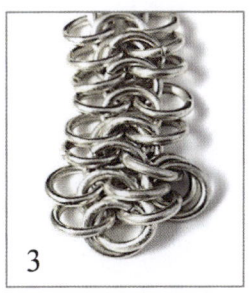

3

Take one open jump ring and scoop the first three bottom jump rings on the right (figure 1) then close the ring (figure 2). Double the ring by running another open jump ring to the first three jump rings just scooped then through to the jump ring just attached to form a knot. Close the ring (figure 3).

STEP FIVE

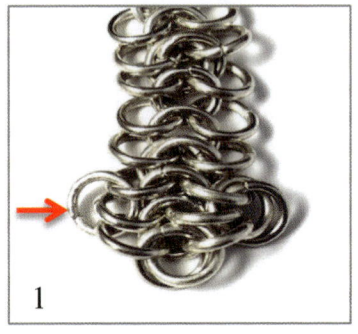

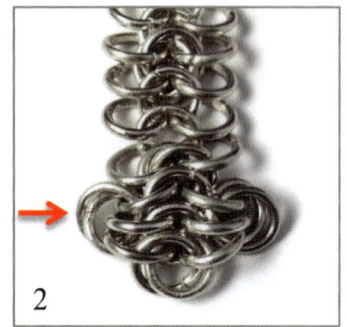

Repeat step four to the opposite row. See figures 1 and 2.

STEP SIX

Repeat steps four and five to finish the whole chain.

STEP SEVEN

At the first end of your chain, attach one jump ring (figure1), double the jump ring by passing through it before closing to form a knot (figure 2). Attach another open jump ring to the knotted rings, and before closing the ring connect it to your lobster clasp (figure 3). Double the ring by forming a knot as you pass through the loop of the lobster clasp. Close the ring (figure 4).

STEP EIGHT

To finish the other end of your chain follow step seven but instead of attaching a lobster clasp, attach eight jump rings, connected one at a time (figure 2). From the 8th jump ring, form a knot by running the three jump rings through it one at a time (figure 3).

chapter four

DRAGONSCALE WEAVE

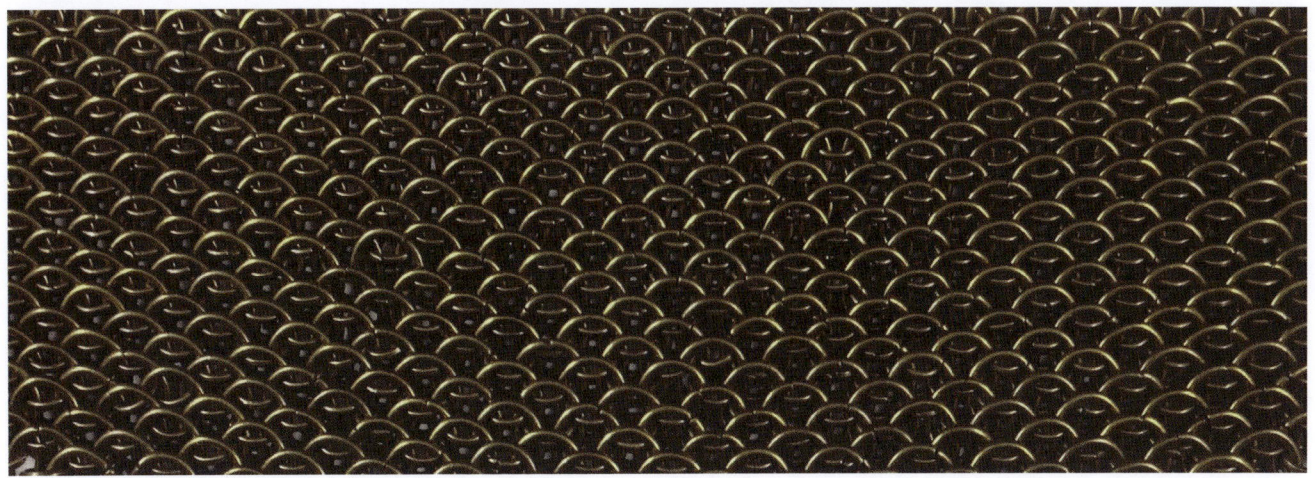

A two ring size weave which consists of a large ring and a small ring. These rings are alternately attached layer by layer thus give the dragonscale effect. It is an intricate weave and is a skill to be learnt by repetition, trial and error. As you practice more often, your skills improve and with patience, this pattern can bring you many beautiful designs in your jewellery collections. So get your two pliers on hand plus your jump rings and get weaving!

STEPS TO FOLLOW

STEP ONE

You need a two size jump ring. One small and one large.

STEP TWO

Make sure your small ring fits inside your large ring.

STEP THREE

Take three closed large jump rings and two open small jump rings. Attach the small open ring to two large rings. Close jump ring. Scoop one large ring with the remaining small open jump ring and attach it to one of the large rings previously attached. Close ring.

STEP FOUR

Arrange your rings. This is your first layer and also the width of your piece. You can make your width wider by adding more jump rings using small and large alternately.

STEP FIVE

Take one closed large jump ring and place it on top of the small ring on the right.

STEP SIX

Take another one closed large jump ring and place it on top of the small ring on the left. This is your second layer.

STEP SEVEN

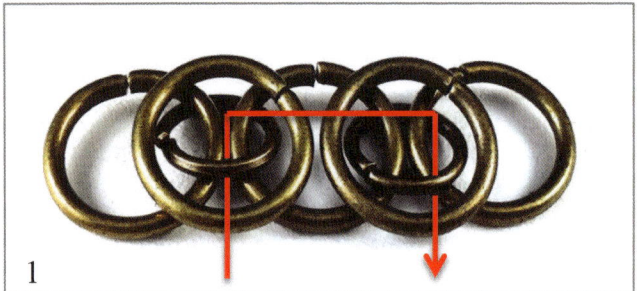

Take one large open jump ring and attach it to the small jump ring on the left and then attach it to the small jump ring on the right. Close the ring. See Figure 1. It should now look like in figure 2.

STEP EIGHT

Take one large open jump ring and attach it to the small jump ring on the right. Close the ring. See Figure 2. Your rings should look like in figure 3.

STEP NINE

Take one open large jump ring and attach it to the small jump ring on the left. Close the ring. See figure 2. Your rings should look like in figure 3. This is your third layer.

STEP TEN

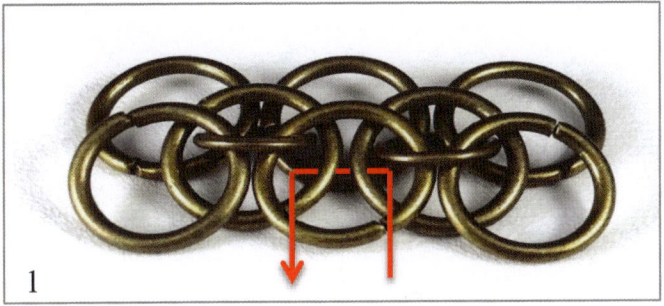 

Take one open small jump ring and attach it to the two large jump rings located behind the large jump ring in the middle. Close the ring. See figure 1. Your ring should look like in figure 2.

NOTE: it's far easier to close your jump rings when linking it to one another by lifting it from the surface. But it's also good to lay them on the table and arrange them after each link to be able to have a more unobstructed view of your pattern especially if you are a beginner to this weave.

STEP ELEVEN

1

2

Take another one small open jump ring and attach it to the large jump ring just behind the large jump ring on the front right. Close the small jump ring. See figure 1. Your rings should now look like figure 2.

STEP TWELVE

1

2

Take another small open jump ring and attach it to the large jump ring just behind the large jump ring on the front left (figure 1). Close the small jump ring. See figure 1. Your rings should now look like figure 2.

STEP THIRTEEN

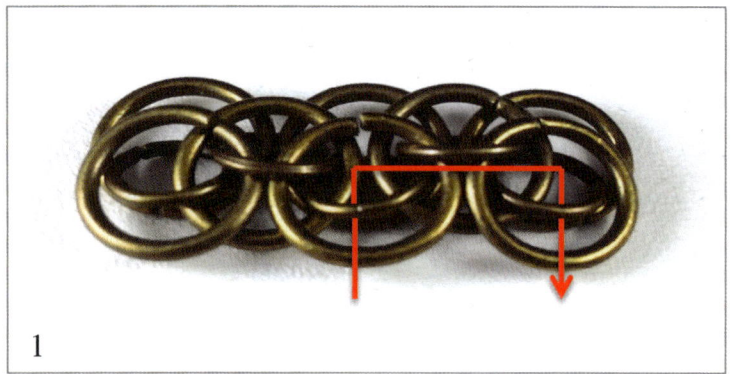

1

2

Take one open large jump ring and pass it through to the small jump ring that is coming out from behind the middle large jump ring then pass it through to the next small jump ring that is coming out from behind the large jump ring on the right. Close the large jump ring. See figure 1. You have now linked the rings as in figure 2.

STEP FOURTEEN

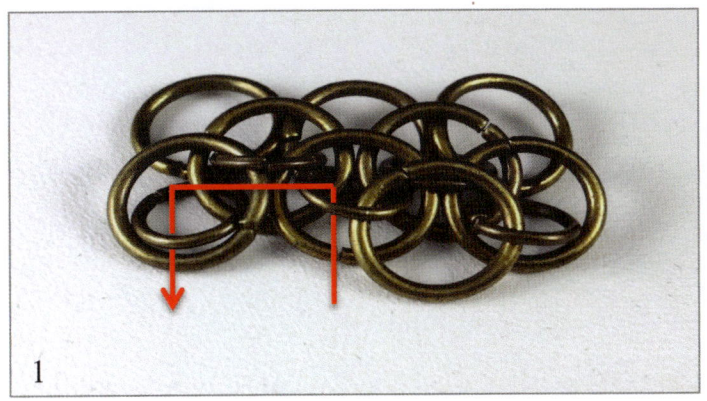

Take one open large jump ring and pass it through to the small jump ring that is coming out from behind the middle large jump ring then pass it through to the next small jump ring that is coming out from behind the large jump ring on the left. Close the large jump ring. See figure 1. Your rings are now linked as in figure 2. This is now your 4th layer.

STEP FIFTEEN

With one open small jump ring, attach the two large jump rings located behind the front large jump ring on the right. Close the small jump ring. See figure 1. Your links should look like in figure 2.

STEP SIXTEEN

With one open small jump ring, attach the two large jump rings located behind the front large jump ring on the left. Close the small jump ring. See figure 1. Your links should look like in figure 2.

STEP SEVENTEEN

- Repeat steps seven-nine to add your 3 large rings.
- Repeat steps ten-twelve to add your 3 small rings.
- Repeat steps thirteen-fourteen to add your 2 large rings.
- Repeat steps fifteen-sixteen to add your 2 small rings.

NOTE: when connecting your large jump rings, you will notice that you are adding them in front of the weave. When connecting your small jump rings, you are adding them at the back of the weave.

STEP EIGHTEEN

Continue adding the layers of your weave by repeating step seventeen. You will now notice that you are just repeating the pattern 3L-3S-2L-2S (3 large jump rings - 3 small jump rings - 2 large jump rings - 2 small jump rings) alternately until you have finished your desired length.

DRAGONSCALE BRACELET

A gorgeous 8 inch long dragonscale bracelet crafted in antique bronze jump rings. The two sizes jump ring difference makes this dragonscale looks very prominent making this bracelet a very elegant piece. The bracelet is suitable for everyday use or equally suited to a special occasion. It is closed safely by a stylish antique bronze toggle clasp.

TO CREATE YOU WILL NEED

197 Large antique bronze jump rings - 5.30mm ID, 20 gauge
197 Small antique bronze jump rings - 3.70mm ID, 22 gauge
2 antique bronze jump rings – 5.70mm ID, 18 gauge
8 antique bronze jump rings – 2.70mm ID, 22 gauge

1 antique bronze toggle clasp
Chain nose pliers
Long nose pliers

I recommend you use two different colour sizes for your jump rings to enable you to work on the structure easier as it can be confusing if you're a first-timer with this weave.

STEPS TO FOLLOW

STEP ONE

Follow steps one-eighteen on pages 88-92 to create your dragonscale bracelet. The width of your bracelet will consist of three large jump rings (5.30mm ID, 20 gauge) and two small jump rings (3.70mm ID, 22 gauge) as arranged in photo above.

STEP TWO

1

2

You will end your bracelet with two small rings coming out from the two large rings. See figures 1 and 2.

STEP TRHREE

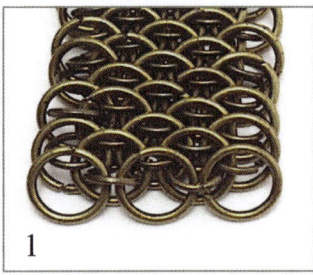 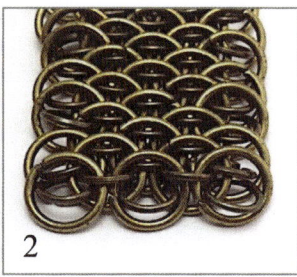 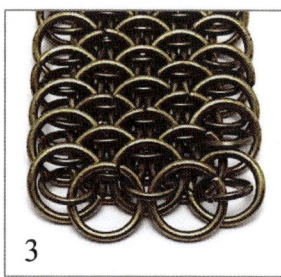 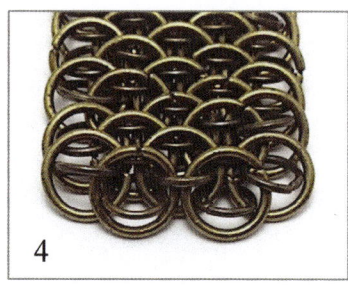

Since you began your weave with three large rings connected by two small rings (figure 1), you now have to attach 3 small rings (figure 2), then 2 large rings (figure 3), followed by 2 small rings (figure 4) to be exactly the same as the other end of the bracelet. Follow steps ten-sixteen on pages 89-91.

STEP FOUR

Take two jump rings (2.70mm ID, 22 gauge) and attach it to the loop of your toggle clasp.

Take one jump ring (5.70mm ID, 18 gauge) and attach it to the two jump rings just attached in figure 1. Before closing the ring, link it to the two small rings at the end of the bracelet. See figures 2 and 3.

STEP FIVE

Take the six remaining jump rings (2.70mm ID, 22 gauge). Attach a pair to the toggle bar, then connect the pair to another pair of jump rings and to another pair. Take one jump ring (5.70mm ID, 18 gauge) and connect it to the last pair of rings and to the two small jump rings from the end of your bracelet.

PINE CONE EARRINGS AND A NECKLACE

A delicate pair of drop earrings and a necklace resembling pine cones which are weaved carefully in an overlapping pattern with black faceted teardrop beads.

TO CREATE YOU WILL NEED

For the Earrings
40 small gunmetal jump rings - 4.65mm ID, 20 gauge
36 large silver plated jump rings - 6.98mm ID, 22 gauge
2 black acrylic faceted teardrop beads

For the Necklace
71 small gunmetal jump rings – 4.65mm ID, 20 gauge
18 large silver plated jump rings - 6.98mm ID, 22 gauge
1 silver plated toggle clasp
1 black acrylic faceted teardrop beads

Chain nose pliers
Flat nose pliers

STEPS TO FOLLOW

EARRINGS

STEP ONE

Start by creating your six dragonscale layers as the main part of your earrings. Follow steps one-eighteen on pages 88-92.

Since you began your weave with three large jump rings (6.98mm ID, 22 gauge) connected by two small rings (4.65mm ID, 20 gauge), you now have to attach three small rings, then two large rings, followed by two small rings to have the same ends. You have just created the seventh layer. Follow steps ten-sixteen on pages 89-91.

STEP TWO

1

2

3

Once you've created your layers, turn it over like the photo shown on figure 1. Take one open gunmetal jump ring and attach it to your ear wire hook (**NOTE: ensure the hook is facing the back of your front piece**) then attach it to the two gunmetal jump rings at the top end of your piece. Pass the open gunmetal jump ring coming from under the first closed gunmetal jump ring then through to the second gunmetal jump ring (figure 2). Close the gunmetal jump ring (figure 3).

STEP THREE

Using your thumb and index finger carefully fold your piece inwards trapping the ear wire hook inside. See figure 1. Take one open gunmetal jump ring and stitch the upper right three large silver plated jump rings to the upper left three silver plated jump rings. Close the ring. The top six large silver plated jump rings are now connected by one small gunmetal jump ring. See figures 3 and 4.

STEP FOUR

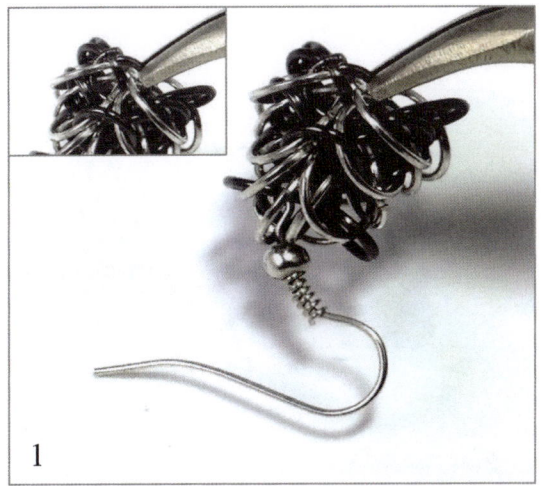

This time, connect the next two lower large silver plated jump rings to the bottom two large silver plated jump rings attached in step three with a small gunmetal jump ring. See figure 2.

STEP FIVE

1

2

3

4

Turn your piece over; this will be the front of your earrings (figure 1). Take one large open silver plated jump ring, and attach it to your teardrop bead then connect it to the two small gunmetal jump rings at the bottom of your piece. Pass the large open silver plated jump ring from under the closed gunmetal jump ring then through to the next closed gunmetal jump ring (figure 3). Close the ring. Repeat steps one-six to finish the other pair of your earring.

NECKLACE

STEP ONE

Create your chain using the gunmetal jump rings. Take one open jump ring and attach it to the clasp's loop then to one closed jump ring. Close the ring. Take another open ring and scoop one closed jump ring, then connect it to the closed jump ring just attached. Close the ring. Repeat process until you have attached all 49 gunmetal jump rings. Before closing the 49th jump ring attach it to the toggle bar.

STEP TWO

Create the main part of your pendant. Weave your dragonscale layers like you did in step one on page 98 to create your earrings. See figure 1. Turn it over and the gunmetal rings are more visible. Now, take your chain and find the middle jump ring or the 25th jump ring. See figure 3.

STEP THREE

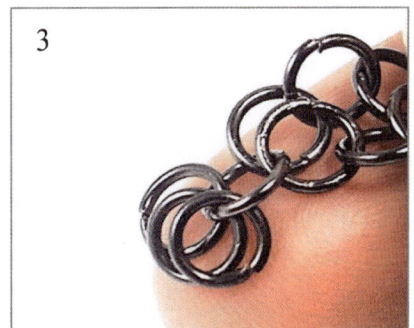

Open the middle jump ring, then attach it to the three closed gunmetal jump rings. Close the ring. See figure 3.

STEP FOUR

Take one open gunmetal jump ring and attach it to the three rings attached to your chain then to the pendant. To do this, pass the open jump ring through the first right top gunmetal ring then through to the left top gunmetal metal ring. Close the ring.

STEP FIVE

Follow steps three-five on pages 99-100 to finish your pendant.

CITRINE ROUGH NUGGETS LANTERN

Weaved by hand with absolute care and attention, this lovely pair of earrings attached to a dragonscale frame with rough citrine nuggets suspended from three spun circles.

TO CREATE YOU WILL NEED

38 Large antique bronze jump rings - 7.81mm ID, 18 gauge
34 Small antique bronze jump rings - 5.05mm ID, 20 gauge
32 antique bronze jump rings - 5.74mm ID, 18 gauge
8 antique bronze jump rings - 3.60mm ID, 21 gauge
6 antique bronze jump rings - 2.69mm ID, 22 gauge

2 silver plated eye pin
4 seed beads
2 rough citrine nugget beads
2 antique bronze ear wire hooks
Chain nose pliers, Flat nose pliers,
Round nose pliers

STEPS TO FOLLOW

STEP ONE

Create the main frame of your earring by weaving dragonscale layers following steps one-eighteen on pages 88-92. End your frame with one large jump ring.

Your layers will consist of 19 large jump rings (7.81mm ID, 18 gauge) and 17 small jump rings (5.05mm ID, 20 gauge).

STEP TWO

1

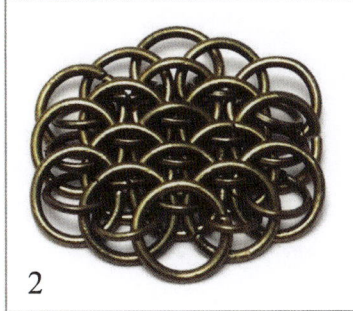

2

Turn your piece over and continue to add some more layers (see steps ten-sixteen on pages 89-91) and end it with one large jump ring. See figures 1 and 2. See also page 109.

STEP THREE

Now take your ear wire hook and two jump rings (2.69mm ID, 22 gauge). Open one jump ring and scoop one closed jump ring and the eye of the ear wire hook. Close jump ring. Now open the last jump ring and attach it to the top large jump ring of your earring frame. Turn your piece over and continue with step four.

STEP FOUR

1

2

3

Using (5.74mm ID, 18 gauge) jump rings, create three sets of Mobius weave with four jump rings on each set. See page 112, steps one and two to create Mobius weave. Now connect these sets with two jump rings. See figure 2. Take one open jump ring and attach it to the first Mobius weave then to the bottom large jump ring of your earring frame. Close jump ring. See figure 3.

STEP FIVE

1

2

3

4

5

6

Take your eye pin, two seed beads and rough citrine nugget beads. Thread a seed bead into your eye pin, followed by your rough citrine nugget bead then finally the last seed bead. Bend your wire above the seed bead at an angle. Take your round nose plier and curl your wire, reposition your plier till you managed to create a loop. Your rough citrine nugget bead and seed beads are now secure.

STEP SIX

Create a Mobius weave using four jump rings (3.60mm ID, 21 gauge). Take one open jump ring (2.69mm ID, 22 gauge) and attach it to the Mobius weave you've just created then to one end of the loop of your stone. See figure 2.

STEP SEVEN

Take one open jump ring (5.74mm ID, 18 gauge) and connect it to the last end of the Mobius weave then to the other end of the loop. You now have created an earring. Repeat steps one-seven to create the other pair.

Try using silver plated eye pin to give contrast with the antique bronze colour and it should work out fine. You can always use the same colour as your jump ring if you prefer it.

DRAGONSCALE FLOWER COLLAR

A beautiful warm antique bronze collar. This elegant piece consisted twelve flower-like dragonscale links and spaced between four copper jump rings all fastened with a stripe carved toggle clasp.

TO CREATE YOU WILL NEED

228 large antique bronze jump rings - 7.81mm ID, 18 gauge
204 small antique bronze jump rings - 5.05mm ID, 20 gauge
56 antique copper jump rings - 2.79mm ID, 22 gauge

Antique bronze toggle and bar clasp
Chain nose pliers
Flat nose pliers

STEPS TO FOLLOW

STEP ONE

Connect three large jump rings (7.81mm ID, 18 gauge) and two small jump rings (5.05mm ID, 20 gauge) as shown in figure 1. This will be the width of your weave.

STEP TWO

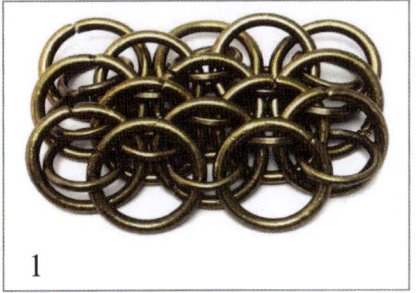
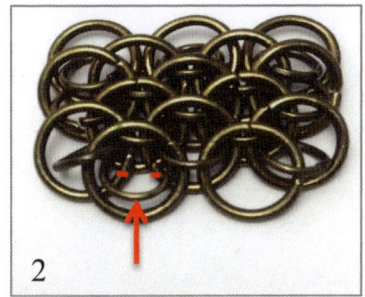
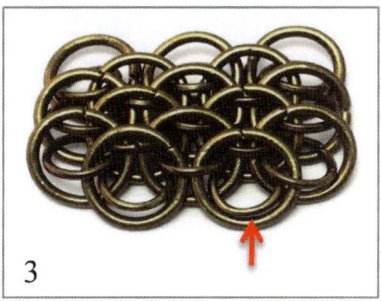

Continue weaving following steps one-eighteen on pages 88-92 until you've reached the sixth layer ending in two large jump rings. See figure 1. Take one small jump ring and attach it to the two large jump rings behind the large jump ring in the front left. See figure 2. Take another small jump ring and connect it to the two large jump rings behind the large jump ring in the front right. See figure 3. Take one large jump ring and link it to the two small jump rings just attached. See figure 4. This will be the first end of your dragonscale flower.

STEP THREE

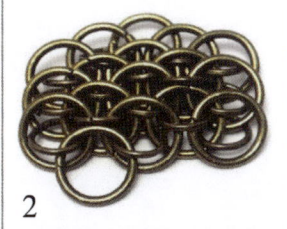

Flip your weave (see figure 1), and you're back to where you started. Connect one large jump ring to the left and middle small jump ring in front of the two large jump rings. See figure 2. Take another large jump ring and connect it to the right and middle small jump ring in front of the two large jump rings. See figure 3. Repeat step two to finish the other end of your dragonscale flower. See figure 4. You have just weaved your first dragonscale flower design. Weave 12 pieces for your collar design.

STEP FOUR

After you have weaved twelve pieces of dragonscale flowers, you can now attach them with each other with four antique copper jump rings (2.79mm ID, 22 gauge). Take one open small antique copper jump ring and connect it to the large jump ring at each end of your flower, then close the ring. Connect three more.

STEP FIVE

Connect the first end of your collar to your toggle clasp. Open the large jump ring and connect it to the loop end of your toggle clasp. Close the jump ring.

STEP SIX

Connect four antique copper jump rings to the other end of your collar. Then attach 8 more antique copper jump rings to the four jump rings just attached. Link two jump rings first followed by the next two until all eight jump rings are connected. Before closing the last pair, attach it to the loop end of your toggle bar then close both rings.

110

chapter five

MOBIUS WEAVE

Another beautiful weave attached to one another like a never-ending circle. It is an easy pattern to follow. Just connect each ring to a set of Mobius to create your beautifully designed jewellery.

STEPS TO FOLLOW

STEP ONE

1

2

3

Start your weave with one closed jump ring. Take one open jump ring and attach it to the closed jump ring. Close the ring. Arrange your rings.

STEP TWO

1

2

3

4

Attach another open jump ring to the two rings just connected in step one. Close the jump ring. Arrange your rings. Continue to form your knot by attaching more rings following steps one and two until you have reached the desired look and thickness.

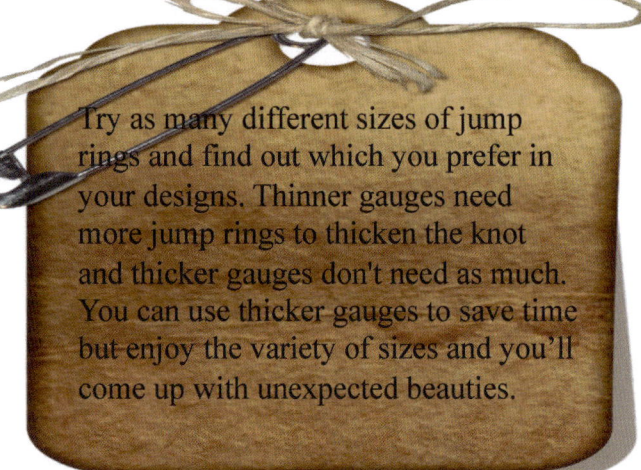

Try as many different sizes of jump rings and find out which you prefer in your designs. Thinner gauges need more jump rings to thicken the knot and thicker gauges don't need as much. You can use thicker gauges to save time but enjoy the variety of sizes and you'll come up with unexpected beauties.

NEST BRACELET WITH RHINESTONE BUTTERFLY CHARMS

Sets of fourteen jump rings of silver beauty, each wrapped together in never ending circles like a nest surrounded by colourful rhinestone butterfly charms finished with a bold silver toggle clasp and a bar. An 8.5 inches versatile and wearable design bracelet.

TO CREATE YOU WILL NEED

18 silver plated jump rings - 5.34mm ID, 17 gauge
28 silver plated jump rings - 6.12mm ID, 19 gauge
98 silver plated jump rings - 10.54mm ID, 20 gauge
3 green rhinestone butterfly charms

3 pink rhinestone butterfly charms
1 silver plated toggle clasp and bar
Chain nose pliers
Flat nose pliers

STEPS TO FOLLOW

STEP ONE

   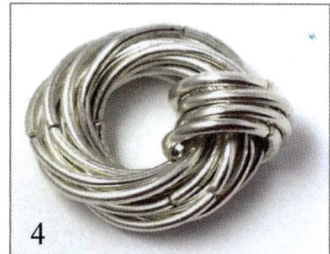

Weave your nest (figure 1) using fourteen jump rings (10.54mm ID, 20 gauge). Follow steps one and two on page 112. Weave seven nests to create the bracelet. Next, attach four jump rings (6.12mm ID, 19 gauge) to the nests (figures 2-4).

STEP TWO

Separate the four rings into two on each side of the nest. Repeat this step to the remaining six nests.

STEP THREE

Take one open jump ring (5.34mm ID, 17 gauge) to connect the two nests together through the pair of jump rings linked on each side (figure 2). Repeat step three until you have attached all the other nests (figure 3).

STEP FOUR

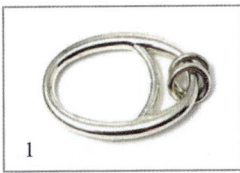 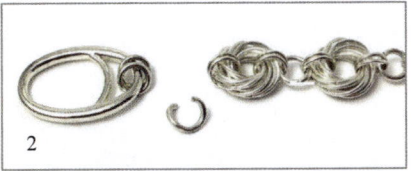 

Attach two jump rings (5.34mm ID, 17 gauge) to your toggle clasp (figure 1). Take another jump ring (5.34mm ID, 17 gauge) and attach it to the first two rings at the end of your bracelet then to the two rings just attached to the toggle clasp (figure 2).

STEP FIVE

  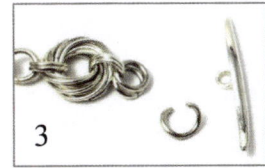 

Take two jump rings (5.34mm ID, 17 gauge) and link it to the two rings attached at the other end of your bracelet (figures 1 and 2) then take another jump ring (5.34mm ID, 17 gauge) and attach it to the two rings just attached and to your toggle bar (figures 3 and 4).

Your bracelet looks like this so far. It is beautiful as it is and you can decide to stop here. Choose stylish closures, and this design itself will stand out.

STEP SIX

Attach one jump ring (5.34mm ID, 17 gauge) to each of your butterfly rhinestone charms (figure 1), then connect each to the jump ring that's attached in between the knots (figures 2 and 3). Alternate the colours.

MOBIUS JEWELLERY SET

MOBIUS LINK BACELET

Each ring weaved on top of each other flowing in one direction gives this beautiful bracelet a stunning look. A 7.75 inch long finished with a stylish silver plated toggle clasp and a bar.

TO CREATE YOU WILL NEED

268 silver plated jump rings - 10.54mm ID, 20 gauge
4 silver plated jump rings - 6.95mm ID, 22 gauge
12 silver plated jump rings - 2.90mm ID, 22 gauge

Chain nose pliers
Flat nose pliers

STEPS TO FOLLOW

STEP ONE

Start by opening all jump rings. You need to create 10 Mobius knots for this bracelet, and each knot is formed of 25 jump rings using the 10.54mm ID, 20 gauge. Make your knots following the steps on page 112. It should look like the photo shown on the left.

STEP TWO

  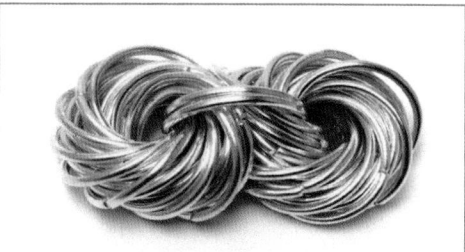

Once you've created all your knots, you now need to connect them using your (10.54mm ID, 20 gauge) jump ring. With an open jump ring join the first two knots. Close the ring. Double the ring. Continue joining each knot to another knot until all ten knots are connected.

STEP THREE

Attach one open (6.95mm ID, 22 gauge) jump ring to your clasp then to the knot at one end of your bracelet. Close the ring. Double the ring.

STEP FOUR

Connect one open (2.90mm ID, 22 gauge) jump ring to your toggle bar then close the ring. Double the ring. Attach another pair of rings to the two rings just attached. Continue with this process until you have connected all the six pair of rings creating a short chain. Take one (6.95mm ID, 22 gauge) open jump ring and attach it to the knot at the other end of your bracelet and the end of the chain. Close the ring. Double the ring.

MOBIUS LINK DANGLY EARRINGS

A stylish and elegant drop earrings (1.75") formed into overlapping circles and suspended from a sterling silver earring wires. These beautiful earrings are a great addition to any outfit.

TO CREATE YOU WILL NEED

50 silver plated jump rings - 10.54mm ID, 20 gauge
28 silver plated jump rings - 1.98mm ID, 24 gauge
4 silver plated jump rings - 6.95mm ID, 22 gauge

2 sterling silver ear wires
Chain nose pliers
Flat nose pliers

STEPS TO FOLLOW

STEP ONE

 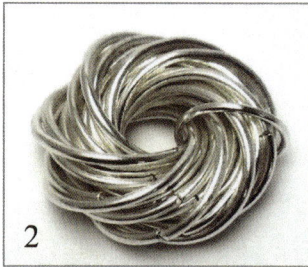 

To begin, create your Mobius knot (figure 1) with 25 jump rings (10.54mm ID, 20 gauge). See page 112 for steps to follow. Next, take one open jump ring (6.95mm ID, 22 gauge) and attach it to your knot. Close the ring (figure 2). Double the ring (figure 3).

STEP TWO

Attach one open jump ring (1.98mm ID, 24 gauge) to the two rings just attached in step one. Close the ring. Double the ring. Repeat this step until you have attached all 14 jump rings. Before closing your last two jump rings, attach it to your ear wire one at a time.

STEP THREE

Repeat steps one-three to create the other pair.

MOBIUS LINK NECKLACE

A Mobius pendant which dangles from a joined S-type silver plated connector chain. Elegant and comfortable to wear. Finished with a silver plated lobster clasp.

TO CREATE YOU WILL NEED

25 silver plated jump rings - 10.54mm ID, 20 gauge
43 silver plated jump rings – 1.98mm ID, 24 gauge
2 silver plated jump rings - 6.70mm ID, 21 gauge
1 silver plated jump ring - 3.17mm ID, 22 gauge
40 S-shape silver plated connectors

1 sterling silver lobster clasp
1 sterling silver jump ring
Chain nose pliers
Flat nose pliers

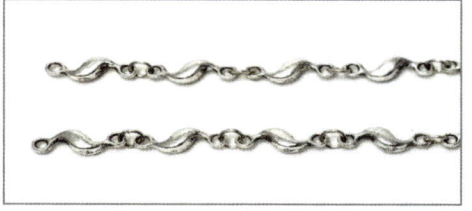

STEPS TO FOLLOW

STEP ONE

Create your Mobius pendant using 25 jump rings (910.54mm ID, 20 gauge). See page 112 for instructions. Attach two jump rings (6.70mm ID, 21 gauge) to secure the weave. Take two jump rings (1.98mm ID, 24 gauge) and attach it to the two jump rings just attached.

STEP TWO

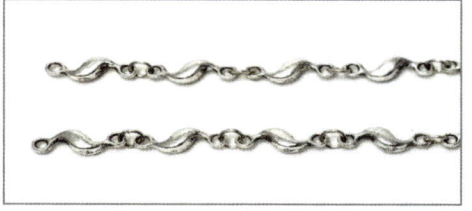

Make two sets of chain by connecting 20 connectors each using 1.98mm ID, 24 gauge jump rings.

STEP THREE

Link each chain to your pendant. Take one (1.98mm ID, 24 gauge) jump ring and attach it to one end of the chain and to the two jump rings attached to the pendant. Repeat this step to attach the other end of chain.

STEP FOUR

Attach a jump ring (10.54mm ID, 20 gauge) to the loop of the lobster clasp and to the first end of chain (figures 1 and 2). Next, attach one jump ring (3.17mm ID, 22 gauge) to the other end of the chain (figures 3and 4).

chapter six

BOX WEAVE

Developed from Byzantine weave, this pattern makes beautiful and great looking chains and many stunning jewellery designs.

Box weave starts the same way as that of Byzantine, and the difference is, the latter has a pair of jump rings linked between each box that gives a gap. The technique used in this weave is the Flip method, whereby you flip a couple of jump rings to attach the next pair of jump rings and so on until you finish the pattern.

Another variation of this pattern is the European 4 in 1 weave. Create the length of your European 4 in 1 chain then you start linking pairs of rings one at a time from one side to the other side to close the flat chain into a box chain. This technique is called the Stitch method.

So, one can have the option to create a design in two ways. The Flip method and the Stitch method. Try both methods and see which you prefer most. I work well with the Flip process and so it's what I've used in the instructions in this chapter.

FLIP METHOD

STEPS TO FOLLOW

STEP ONE

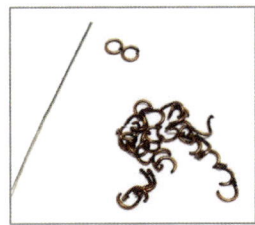 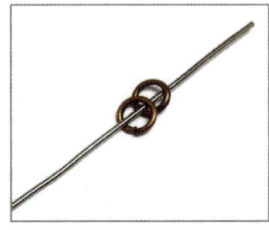 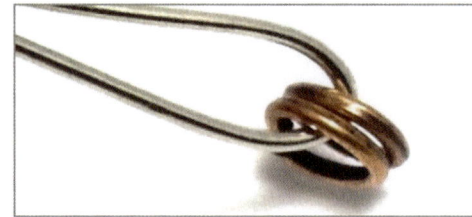

Prepare two closed jump rings, lots of open jump rings and a piece of wire to help you hold your weave as well as to mark your starting point. To begin, scoop the two closed jump rings with your piece of wire then fold the wire, trapping the two closed jump rings.

STEP TWO

Take one open jump ring and attach it to the two closed jump rings. Close the jump ring. Double the jump ring.

STEP THREE

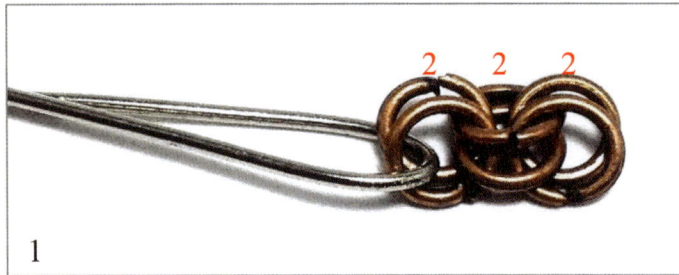 

Take another open jump ring and connect it to the two jump rings just attached in step two. Double the ring. Notice the 2-2-2 pattern. See figure 1. Arrange your rings (figure 2).

STEP FOUR

Now, you have to flip back the last two jump rings on each side. Flip back the top one on its side first. See figure 1. Next, flip back the bottom one on its side. See figure 2.

STEP FIVE

Once you have flipped back the last two jump rings, the middle two jump rings appear. Open the rings wide and the two tails of the last two jump rings just flipped back in step four appears. See figure 2. You have just weaved your first box.

STEP SIX

To continue weaving your box, take one open jump ring and attach it to the two rings. Close the ring. Double the ring. Your first box is also now completely secured.

STEP SEVEN

Take another open jump ring and attach it to the two rings. Close the jump ring. Double the jump ring. You'll again notice a 2-2-2 pattern like in step 3.

STEP EIGHT

Again, flip back the two jump rings on each side, then the middle two jump rings appear. Open the rings, and the tail of the two jump rings that was previously flipped back now emerged. Connect a jump ring and double the jump ring. Continue the pattern following steps seven and eight until you have reached your desired length.

STITCH METHOD

STEPS TO FOLLOW

STEP ONE

Weave your European 4-in-1 chain. Follow steps one-five on pages 44-45 for the detailed instructions. Decide the length and width of your chain.

STEP TWO

1

2

Begin stitching your flat chain. Take your open jump ring and link it to the second bottom jump ring and passing it through to the first bottom jump ring. Pass your ring on top of the first jump ring in the middle row then you continue linking it to the first top jump ring through to the second top jump ring. Close the ring. See figures 1 and 2.

STEP THREE

1

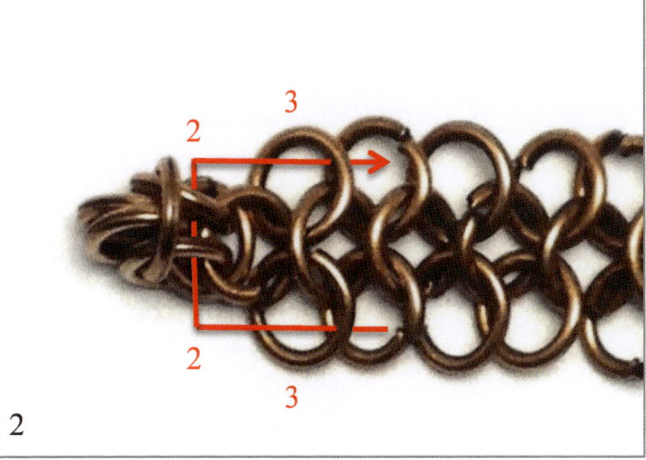

2

3

Stitch the next pair of jump rings. First, lift the middle top jump ring (figure 1). Take your open jump ring and pass it to the bottom third jump ring and the bottom second folded jump ring. Continue passing it through the top second folded jump ring then through to the top third jump ring. Close the ring. See figures 2 and 3.

STEP FOUR

Repeat step three until you have stitched all the remaining pairs of jump rings.

GRADUATED MESH COLLAR WITH PEARLS

A lovely antique bronze box weave necklace accented with freshwater pearls. Finished securely with a stylish J hook and eye clasp.

TO CREATE YOU WILL NEED

412 antique bronze jump rings - 4.60mm ID, 20 gauge
4 large antique bronze jump rings - 7.80mm ID, 18 gauge
28 silver plated jump rings - 2.83mm ID, 22 gauge
7 Silver plated eye pins
7 Freshwater pearls (9mm)
J hook and eye clasp
A piece of wire
Chain nose pliers
Flat nose pliers
Round nose pliers
Side cutters

STEPS TO FOLLOW

STEP ONE

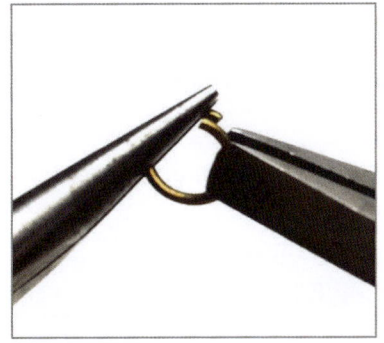 

Before you start, open all jump rings. This will make your work flow smoothly. Thread your seven freshwater pearls with your silver plated eye pins. Follow steps one-four on page 16 to form a simple loop.

STEP TWO

Take your J hook clasp and attach six jump rings (4.60mm ID, 20 gauge) following a 2-2-2 pattern. See figure 1. Weave thirteen boxes. Follow steps one-eight on pages 124-125 to create a box weave.

STEP THREE

At the end of the last box, attach a large jump ring (7.80mm ID, 18 gauge). This now secures your 13th box.

STEP FOUR

Now attach seven boxes. Start creating your boxes by connecting it to the large jump ring (7.80mm ID, 18 gauge) attached in step three.

After you have weaved your seven boxes, secure the last box by connecting a jump ring then double the jump ring.

Take another large jump ring (7.80mm ID, 18 gauge) and attach it to the doubled jump rings just attached.

STEP FIVE

After having attached the large ring in step four, connect six jump rings in a 2-2-2 pattern then create six boxes. Secure your last box with a jump ring. Double the jump ring. Now, take your first freshwater pearl with a loop on each side. Connect the first end loop of your pearl to a pair of silver plated jump rings (2.83mm ID, 22 gauge) then link them to the last couple of jump rings attached to the chain. See figure 3.

STEP SIX

Take one silver plated jump ring and attach it to the other end loop of the pearl. Double the jump ring. Like in step five, connect six antique bronze jump rings in a 2-2-2 pattern to the two silver plated jump rings just attached. Continue creating another six boxes. Secure the last box with an antique bronze jump ring and double the jump ring.

130

STEP SEVEN

Repeat step six to connect your second and third pearl and the six boxes weaved respectively.

STEP EIGHT

Take your large jump ring and attach it to the last pair of jump rings at the end of the chain.

STEP NINE

Weave seven boxes. Start from attaching six jump rings at the large jump ring and follow a 2-2-2 pattern. Secure your last box by attaching another large jump ring.

STEP TEN

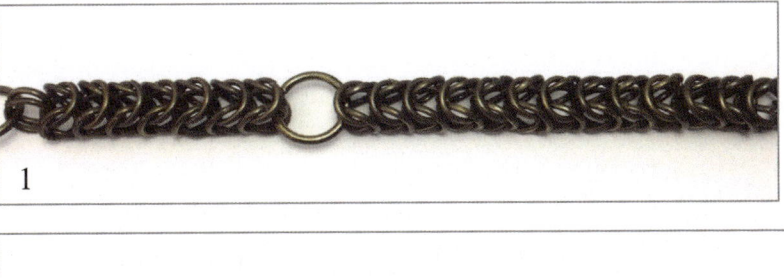 

Weave thirteen boxes. Secure the last box. To do this, take one open jump ring and link it to the two tail ends of the box and then to the loop of your eye clasp before closing the jump ring. Double the jump ring. You have just finished weaving your first length of the collar.

STEP TEN

Attach your next length of collar to the first large jump ring of the finished chain. See figure 1. Begin by connecting six jump rings in a 2-2-2 pattern and weave two boxes. Secure your last box with two jump rings. See figure 2. Take your first threaded pearl secured in two loops. Attach the first loop of pearl to the two jump rings just attached with two silver plated jump rings. See figure 3.

STEP ELEVEN

Attach two silver plated jump rings to the other end loop of pearl then connect six antique bronze jump rings in a 2-2-2 pattern and weave ten boxes. Secure your last box with two jump rings.

Attach the second pearl by connecting it's first loop to the two jump rings just attached with two silver plated jump rings.

Connect two silver plated jump rings at the other end loop of pearl and then attach six antique bronze jump rings in 2-2-2 pattern and weave four boxes. Secure the last box with two antique bronze jump rings then take the third pearl and attach its first end loop to the two antique bronze jump rings with two silver plated jump rings.

STEP TWELVE

Again, attach two silver plated jump rings to the other end loop of the third pearl and then attach six antique bronze jump rings in a 2-2-2 pattern. Weave ten boxes this time and secure the last box with two jump rings. Take your fourth pearl and connect it to the two jump rings just attached with two silver plated jump rings. See figure 1. Take two silver plated jump rings and attach it to the other end loop of the fourth pearl. Now attach six antique jump rings in a 2-2-2 pattern and weave two boxes. Secure the last box with two jump rings. See fig. 2.

STEP THIRTEEN

Before closing the last two jump rings in step twelve, connect it to the large jump ring at the other end of your first weaved collar and close both rings. You have just completed creating your graduated mesh collar with pearls.

TUNNEL CHAIN NECKLACE

An intricate and spellbinding tunnel chain necklace crafted from antique bronze jump rings. Its beautiful, simple box weave design makes it an excellent statement piece.

TO CREATE YOU WILL NEED

282 antique bronze jump rings – 3.67mm ID, 21 gauge
48 antique bronze jump rings - 5.45mm ID, 20 gauge
48 antique bronze jump rings - 5.71mm ID, 18 gauge
36 antique bronze jump rings - 7mm ID, 19 gauge

1 J-hook and eye clasp
Chain nose pliers
Flat nose pliers

STEPS TO FOLLOW

STEP ONE

Start creating your box weave chain using your 122 jump rings (3.67mm ID, 21 gauge). Follow steps one-eight on pages 124-125. Use your hook clasp to hold your weave as well as a starting point of the weave instead of a piece of wire or paper clip. You now have weaved a chain of 30 boxes.

STEP TWO

Link your eight jump rings (5.45mm ID, 20 gauge) starting at the last two tail ends of the chain creating two boxes.

STEP THREE

This time link your eight jump rings (5.71mm ID, 18 gauge) creating another two boxes.

STEP FOUR

Attach your twelve jump rings (7mm ID, 19 gauge) creating three boxes.

STEP FIVE

Like in step three, link another eight jump rings (5.71mm ID, 18 gauge) to create two boxes.

STEP SIX

Like in step two, link another eight jump rings (5.45mm ID, 20 gauge) to create two boxes.

The shape of your chain should now look like photo on left.

STEP SEVEN

Using your twenty jump rings (3.67mm ID, 21 gauge), start connecting it to the last two tail ends of the chain creating 5 boxes.

STEP EIGHT

Continue weaving your chain by repeating steps two-six to create another set of a tunnel-shaped chain.

STEP NINE

STEP TEN

Like in step one, continue weaving your chain by attaching the remaining 120 jump rings (3.67mm ID, 21 gauge).

Repeat steps seven and eight.

STEP ELEVEN

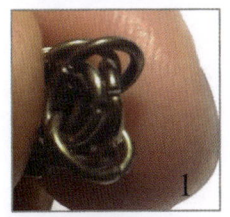

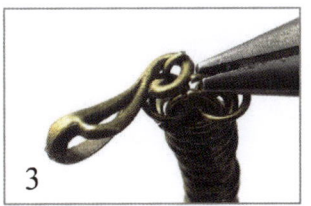

Once you have attached the last two pairs of jump rings in step ten, flip it back. Open one ring that was just flipped back and attach it to the loop of your eye clasp. Close the ring. Repeat it with the other ring. Your finished chain is now ready to wear.

TRIPLE STRAND BRACELET

A lovely three strand bracelet of carefully weaved jump rings with each strand made in the same length for an elegant fit and securely fastened with a filigree copper plated box clasp with clear rhinestones.

TO CREATE YOU WILL NEED

630 copper plated jump rings - 1.94mm ID, 24 gauge
1 copper plated triple strand push button clasp

Flat nose pliers
Chain nose pliers

STEPS TO FOLLOW

STEP ONE

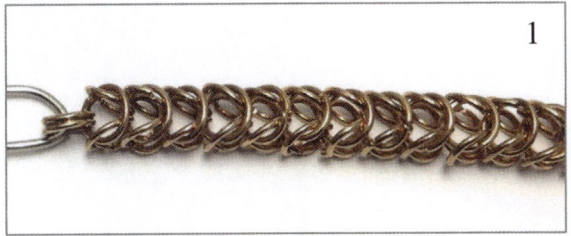

Weave three strands of chain. Use 210 jump rings to create each strand following steps one-eight on pages 124-125. At the end of each chain, just attach the four jump rings, a pair each, and you don't need to flip back the last pair. See figure 2. For each chain you'll weave 51 boxes.

STEP TWO

After having weaved your three strands of chain, take your clasp and attach the first three ends of your chain. Ensure that all ends are looking the same before attaching it to the clasps. Now take each chain and connect it to the other end of your clasp. Before attaching it, make sure that your chain isn't twisted. It can be a little tricky as each side of the chain can be confusing and almost look the same.

INVERTED CONE DANGLY EARRINGS

A sleek and striking pair of graduated long gold earrings that will look fantastic in any style.

TO CREATE YOU WILL NEED

22 gold plated jump rings - 1.90mm ID, 24 gauge
24 gold plated jump rings - 2.80mm ID, 22 gauge
32 gold plated jump rings - 3.51mm ID, 22 gauge
40 gold plated jump rings - 3.90mm ID, 19 gauge
14 gold plated jump rings - 7.80mm ID, 22 gauge

2 gold plated ear wire hooks
Chain nose pliers
Flat nose pliers

STEPS TO FOLLOW

STEP ONE

  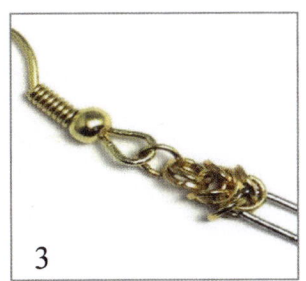

Take one open jump ring (1.90mm ID, 24 gauge) and attach it to your ear wire hook. Close the ring. Using ten jump rings of the same size, weave two boxes linked to the first jump ring previously attached. Follow the pattern in pages 124-125 steps three to eight.

STEP TWO

This time connect twelve jump rings (2.80mm ID, 22 gauge) to continue weaving and slowly widening the shape of your earring creating three boxes of this ring size.

STEP THREE

Continue weaving using 16 jump rings (3.51mm ID, 22 gauge) creating four boxes of this ring size.

STEP FOUR

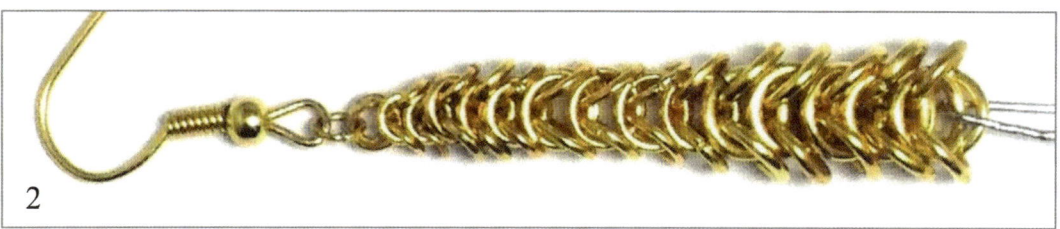

Attach 20 jump rings (3.90mm ID, 19 gauge) as you continue your weave creating five boxes of this ring size.

STEP FIVE

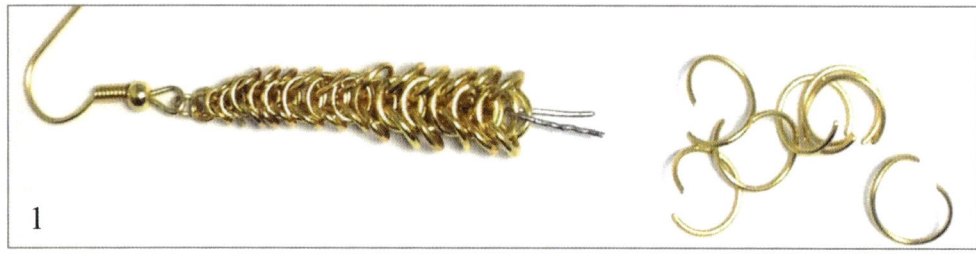

To finish the length of your earring attach seven jump rings (7.80mm ID, 22 gauge) one at a time as you weave it into a Mobius knot. (see page 112, steps one-two). Repeat steps one-five to continue with the other pair.

PEACOCK EARRINGS

A beautiful pair of gold hoops in a box weave design. It's ideal for everyday wear.

TO CREATE YOU WILL NEED

220 gold plated jump rings - 2.80mm ID, 22 gauge
28 gold plated jump rings - 1.90mm ID, 24 gauge
2 gold plated ear wire hooks
Flat nose pliers
Chain nose pliers
2 pieces of wire

STEPS TO FOLLOW

STEP ONE

Using (2.80mm ID, 22 gauge) jump rings, weave your chain following the steps on pages 124-125. Take one jump ring (1.90mm ID, 24 gauge) and connect it to the last end of your chain. Close the ring. Double the ring. Take another piece of wire and attach it to the last two jump rings just connected.

STEP TWO

Now, let each end of the chain meet together. From the first end of your chain, re-open one jump ring (2.80mm ID, 22 gauge) and carefully connect it to the two jump rings (1.90mm ID, 24 gauge) attached previously at the other end of the chain in step one. Close the ring. Repeat procedure to double the ring.

STEP THREE

1

2

3

4

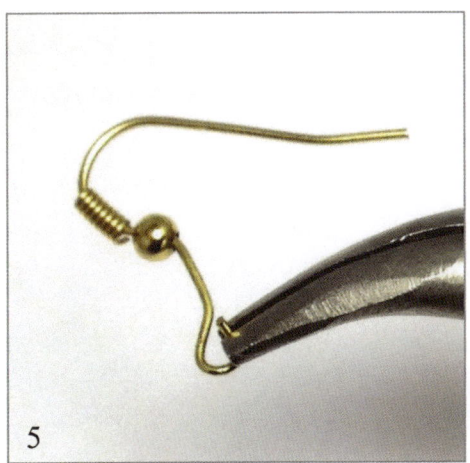

5

6

7

Take one jump ring (1.90mm ID, 24 gauge) and attach it to the two jump rings that were previously re-opened and connected to the two rings in step 2. Close the ring. Double the ring. Link another pair and weave one box. Weave two more boxes. Take your ear wire hook and open the loop then connect it to the two tail ends of the last two jump rings flipped. Close the loop. You now have finished one earring. Repeat steps one-three to create the other pair.

143

BRACELET

A uniquely designed bracelet, crafted from two designs of link. This gorgeous bracelet exhibits alternating golden Box weaved rings and Mobius weaved rings. It is finished with two golden lobster clasp.

TO CREATE YOU WILL NEED

96 small gold plated jump rings chain nose pliers - 2.80mm ID, 22 gauge
80 medium gold plated jump rings flat nose pliers -) 3.51mm ID, 22 gauge
20 large gold plated jump rings - 3.90mm ID, 19 gauge
12 extra large gold plated jump rings - 7.80mm ID, 22 gauge

2 gold plated lobster clasp
A piece of wire
Chain nose pliers
Flat nose pliers

STEPS TO FOLLOW

STEP ONE

Start weaving your bracelet following steps one-eight on pages
124-125. To create the shape of your pattern, start with ten small
jump rings (2.80mm ID, 22 gauge) and weave two boxes.
Followed by eight medium jump rings (3.51mm ID, 22 gauge) to
weave another two boxes. Then the four large jump rings
(3.90mm ID, 19 gauge) to weave just one box. This time,
connect the eight medium jump rings (3.51mm ID, 22 gauge) to
make two boxes followed by the eight small jump rings (2.80mm
ID, 22 gauge) to make another two boxes.

STEP TWO

Take one extra large jump ring (7.80mm ID, 22 gauge) and connect it to the last pair of small rings weaved in step one. Attach another extra large jump ring and weave it into a Mobius knot (see page 112 steps one-two). Repeat with one more extra large jump ring.

STEP THREE

1

This pattern is your first set. Weave the next four sets repeating steps one and two. As you finished weaving each set, link it to the previous one to form your bracelet. See figures 2-4.

2

3

4

STEP FOUR

1

2

3

For the last set, instead of connecting a knot with three extra large jump rings, connect two small jump rings as shown in figure 1. Take another small open jump ring and scoop the lobster clasp then attach it to the last pair of jump rings. Close the ring. Double the ring.

STEP FIVE

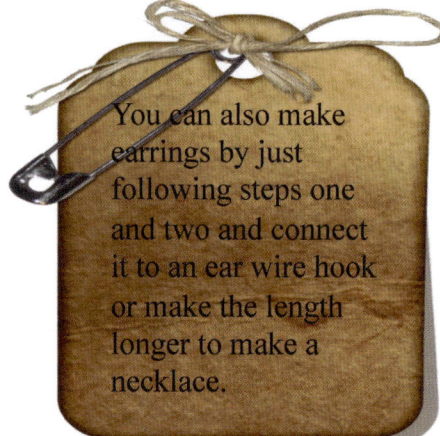

You can also make earrings by just following steps one and two and connect it to an ear wire hook or make the length longer to make a necklace.

Take the other end of your bracelet and attach it to the lobster clasp with two small jump rings.

GOLD FEATHER EARRINGS

Box weaved jump rings in featherlike earrings that will glisten and shine in the breeze.

TO CREATE YOU WILL NEED

60 gold plated jump rings - 3.48mm ID, 22 gauge
14 gunmetal jump rings - 5.28mm ID, 21 gauge
2 gold plated ear wire hooks

Flat nose pliers
Chain nose pliers

STEPS TO FOLLOW

STEP ONE

  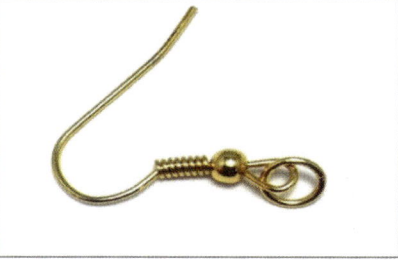 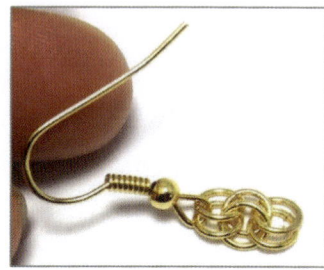

Start creating your earring following steps one and two on page 124. Instead of using a piece of wire, use the ear wire hook to hold your design and to mark your starting point.

STEP TWO

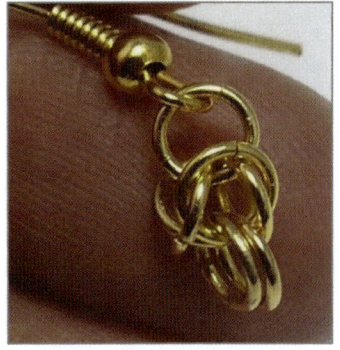  

Continue following steps three-eight on pages 124-125 to finish the length of your earring by weaving seven boxes using 30 gold plated jump rings.

STEP THREE

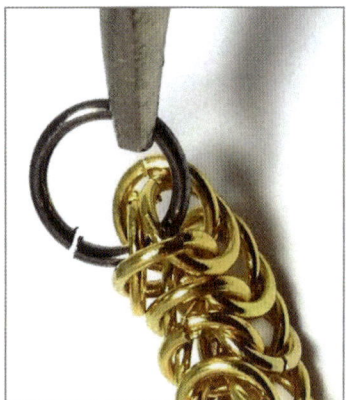  

Link the seven gunmetal jump rings one at a time at the two tail ends of the gold plated jump rings. Repeat steps one-three to create the other pair.

Printed in Great Britain
by Amazon

39400629R00087